ARTISTS
IN THEIR
OWN
WORDS

Also by Paul Cummings

American Drawings: The Twentieth Century

Dictionary of Contemporary American Artists

Fine Arts Market Place

ARTISTS IN THEIR OWN WORDS

INTERVIEWS BY PAUL CUMMINGS

St. Martin's Press
New York

For information, write:
St. Martin's Press, Inc., 175 Fifth Ave., New York, N.Y. 10010.
Manufactured in the United States of America

Library of Congress Cataloging in Publication Data

Cummings, Paul.
Artists in their own words.

1. Artists—United States—Interviews. 2. Artists—United States—Biography. 3. Art, Modern—20th century—United States. I. Title.
N6512.C85 709'.2'2 [B] 79-16474
ISBN 0-312-05512-9

To Gale Garnett

ACKNOWLEDGMENTS

Many people have contributed to the making of this book. To begin with, I wish to express my gratitude to Butler Coleman, who, a dozen years ago, asked me to conduct interviews for the Archives of American Art. His generous, unfailing support during our years at that institution made the experience exceptionally rewarding. To William E. Woolfenden, director of the Archives, my thanks for his aid during the decade of our association.

I am especially grateful to the artists who have graciously permitted portions of these interviews to be published: Ivan Albright, Isamu Noguchi, Kenneth Noland, Philip Pearlstein, Lucas Samaras, and Carl Andre, at whose suggestion this book was undertaken; and to the representatives of artists' estates: John Gorton of the Rockwell Kent Legacies, Lyman Field for Thomas Hart Benton, Irvine Shubert for Katherine Schmidt, Frances Lindley for Walker Evans, Nancy Holt for Robert Smithson, and Mrs. Fairfield Porter for her husband.

A note of appreciation is due the many museums, photographers, art dealers, and individuals who supplied photographs and information: Hugh J. Gourley III, Colby College Art Museum; The Pace Gallery; John Weber Gallery; Sidney Janis Gallery; Sperone Westwater Fischer, Inc.; Anita Duquette, The Whitney Museum of American Art; Helen B. Morrison; Iris Krenzis, Hammer Gallery; Mrs. Percy Uris; Russell Lynes; Renate Ponsold; André Emmerich Gallery; Rudolph Burckhardt; David Gahr; Marian Powers, Time Inc.; Leonard Boudin; Mrs. Bella Fishko; The Weyhe Gallery; Richard K. Larcada; The Zabriski Gallery; Jerry L. Thompson; The Solomon R.

Guggenheim Museum; Diane Waldman; and The Allan Frumkin Gallery.

A particular debt of gratitude is owed to Joan Sumner Ohrstrom for her understanding and her persistently charitable editorial aid and insight, to Louise E. Halsey for her quick, expert typing of almost illegible transcripts, and to Leslie Pockell, my editor at St. Martin's Press, for his continuing encouragement and enthusiasm.

PC
February, 1979,
New York City

CONTENTS

INTRODUCTION

Soon after its founding, the Archives of American Art (now a bureau of the Smithsonian Institution) began conducting interviews with artists, dealers, curators, collectors, museum directors, patrons, and others dedicated to the fine arts. Today, when the contents once committed to a diary or a narrative letter are communicated by a quick telephone call, interviews often constitute the only surviving first-person statement of many individuals. In this age of the on-the-spot reporter and the instant display of events on television, few people are mike shy. Uncommitted to the historic finality of the written word, conversation falls easily into the microphone. The artists' words augment their visual statements.

The most readily abused documentary instrument is the tape-recorded interview. Captured in the instant, the word becomes tangible history upon transcription. The potential insights of traditional biographical inquiry are lost in the speed of electronic efficiency. The spoken word, evaluated at leisure, poses problems different from those of the written document. Conversational and written vocabularies differ. In the ease of quick conversation, the refinement of editing is lacking. Roughly formulated sentences, abrupt stops and starts, the desired word not found, momentary memory lapses—all contribute problems. Nevertheless, the well-conducted interview should provide information and manifest the personality of the individual.

Where one was born and educated; one's family, teachers, friends, travels; the first vivid experiences of art; the first evidence of skill or that moment when the child's drawing becomes something more than play or a way to discover the visible world—all experience affects the artist's formation. Frequently, art grows from drawing. The child's lines and scribbles are transformed into watercolors or paintings; lumps of clay or mud become objects desirous of form. A talent emerges, and its daily exercise becomes imperative. Often a survivor of a rigorous, restricted childhood, the artist bursts forth in maturity with the dream that is art. Through craft and skill, the vision slowly unfolds; the artist, committed to expression, seeks to impress his dream upon our lives.

How does the interviewer elicit the tale of the artist's life? The unstructured interview was developed at Columbia University after World War II for the purpose of recording the memoirs of political and military figures. Long lists of specific, carefully researched questions yielded insufficient information. A narrative discussion of several topics conducted by an informed interviewer produced a considerably more valuable response. Beginning with generalizations, conversation, at first focused on the subject's background, would become increasingly specific. Fully planned interrogation limits free association, and questions focused in anticipation of eliciting particular revelations are constricting. The loaded question, directed toward proving a theory, will appear increasingly shallow in the persistent evaluation of time. Delving into many areas of the subject's life, the listening questioner considers, probes gently, pursues, pushes for more explanations, more data, more evaluations. This method stimulates free association and allows, indeed, encourages, digression. It also demonstrates the treachery of memory. During those moments when the mind is free, and thoughts, memories, and images emerge unencumbered, the interviewer should be aware of what is transpiring and nurture it, continue it, expand it. Because moments of great feeling are often revealed in the early sessions, their value as seminal points remains throughout the interview as a guide in our understanding of the individual. There is little information concerning the artist that is not of interest.

Interviews are best conducted when the interviewee is at ease; with most artists, it is in the studio. Preparation for the interview should include researching previous interviews (to avoid unnecessarily repetitive questions), reading all the writings by or about the artist, and a personal evaluation of his work. Occasionally friends and associates are briefly questioned. As a guide, the interviewer should prepare a chronology and lists of individuals to be mentioned and topics to be discussed, such as art theories, public events, works of art, and general biographical information. The more hours taped, the more rewarding the interview. Thus, a ten-hour interview is more than five times better than a two-hour interview. The time between sessions allows the subconscious to react to the process, and the memory, thus stimulated, will deliver more information during later sessions.

Biographical interviews produce commentary on a variety of subjects other than those immediately concerning the subject. We learn about fads and fashions in art and life and about topics such as politics, economics, science, and language. Above all, the personality of the interviewee should emerge, an understanding of which often leads to a more rewarding experience of his art.

The interviews in this book have been edited from longer versions in the Archives of American Art. Portions of the Katherine Schmidt, Fairfield Porter, and Rockwell Kent interviews were published in the *Archives of American Art Journal* during my editorship. The illustrations have been chosen to reflect the world of each individual and to provide some representation of his art. The variety of experience set forth in the interviews demonstrates the diverse and complex contribution to our cultural heritage of these artists. The insights developed by these individuals' imaginative perception of art and life enrich our heritage. During these decades the American artist emerged on the international scene, secure in his accomplishments, which continue into the third generation. The interviews were edited to reflect the life and ideas of each individual rather than in support of any critical theory. The organization is by birthdate.

PC
January, 1979

Rockwell Kent aboard ship to Tierra del Fuego, 1922. Rockwell Kent Papers, Archives of American Art, Smithsonian Institution, Washington, D.C.

ROCKWELL KENT

1

Rockwell Kent's elegant style was immediately evident, not only in his speech, writings, and art, but in his way of living as well. As one of the last of the many generations to be influenced by the literary style of the King James version of the Bible, Kent (1882–1971) may have rejected its religious message, but its stylistic imprint was evident both in his conversation and in his writing. In this interview, conducted February 26 and 27, 1969, at his home in Au Sable Forks, New York, Kent emerges as a man who clearly enjoyed farming, travel, writing, drawing, politics, designing and producing books, and designing and building houses. Unlike Thomas Hart Benton (q.v.), who could not sustain an intellectual position, Kent remained an intellectual, but, like many patrician Americans, distrusted this aspect of his nature. Needing an alliance with the common man to validate his actions, especially his cultural accomplishments, he utilized his artistic skills to ornament the ideas he expressed in books and pamphlets and through social organizations. He developed a painting and drawing style early in life and maintained it brilliantly. In synthesizing elements of the styles of William Blake, William M. Chase, and art deco, he achieved a style of refreshing personal flair. Kent's innate sense of graphic design expressed through a dramatic use of black and white served him well, not only in his prints, bookplates, and commercial art projects, but in the bold structures of his paintings as well. An agile mind constructed the illustrated letters that were translated into the manuscripts for his travel books.

Kent reveled in the stimulation of confrontation as a mental exercise, rarely as an expression of aggression. Life, he felt, should be a productive, pleasurable experience. He discusses his enjoyment of the cold climes of the world, of contending with nature. Though dedicated to social reform, class distinctions were important to him, even necessary, for they enabled him to have the clear vision of his fellowman he so forcefully expressed in his political actions and in the vast collection of his correspondence now in the Archives of American Art, Smithsonian Institution. He was as proud of his honorary membership (along with only two others at the time, Martin Luther King and Paul Robeson) in the International Longshoremen's Association, as he was of his books, architecture, or art. Despite his many creative accomplishments, Kent objected to being called an artist. He was, rather, "a man who made pictures." His art, an aspect of his nature with which he was uncomfortable, was a creative stimulus for his other activities. A dynamic figure in the history of American culture, Kent's idealism was expressed through his myriad achievements and boundless enthusiasm for life, nature, and people. Succeeding generations will always find appealing qualities in his work.

We were of New England stock, English to start with. That is, the Kents and the Rockwells. My father's father came to New York. He went to Union College. I think my father was born in Brooklyn. By that time the family had a good deal of wealth, so my father went to Harvard, to Yale, to either Fribourg or Heidelberg in Germany, where he got his degree as a mining engineer. Then he came back and went to Columbia Law School and became a lawyer. He kept up his interest in mining and had interests in Honduras. On a trip to Honduras he caught typhoid fever and died when I was six years old, leaving almost nothing. So my mother had a tough time bringing up her family of three children, one of them born after my father's death. But somehow, partly through the friendship and help of her relatives, but mostly through her own and her sister's needlework, cooking, things that could be sold at the Woman's Exchange, she managed to put us through school. None of us ever went to public schools. We always went to private schools, which in those days were considered the only place to send children. Eventually I won a scholarship to Columbia. When I was about fourteen, I went to the Horace Mann School in New York and from there to Columbia, where I studied architecture. I didn't take a degree because in the meantime I decided—I had been studying painting in the summer under William M. Chase at Shinnecock—I decided that I wanted to become a painter and not an architect, despite my mother's and her sister's warning that, "You'll never be able to support yourself as an artist—nobody can." So I switched at the beginning of my junior year and began to study art at night at the Chase school, which later became the Henri school, while I continued another year at Columbia.

Why did you pick Chase to study with?

Well, I would go to Long Island in the summertime. Some summers I worked in the Tarrytown National Bank. And I was showing interest enough in art so that the family decided they could send me to Shinnecock. In the meantime, my mother and my aunt together had bought a cottage in what was then called the art village, which was built around the big studio where Chase conducted his classes. So I began going down there and did very well. Then I was awarded a scholarship, which went on from year to year, at the Chase school in New York. Finally, I was listed as an instructor there, though I was never called upon to instruct. So my art education, aside from the earliest years at Shinnecock under Chase, cost nobody anything.

You had no other art training prior to that?

No. I drew at home. My Aunt Josephine painted china to sell at the Woman's Exchange, and I took to painting china and making other things of that sort. Burnt leather work, too. I became an expert at it.

You started drawing very early then.

Oh, yes. About thirteen. But all children start drawing young. And with encouragement, many of them would keep on doing it. All my children used to love to draw pictures. When I came back from Alaska, where I lived for a year with my eight-year-old son, I had a big exhibition of drawings at Knoedler's and showed his drawings, four or five of them—naive children's drawings. All of them were bought at a fairly good price for a kid, twenty-five dollars each maybe, by Arthur B. Davies. Then, a couple of years later, at the big Independents Show at the Grand Central Palace, I showed more of his pictures—bigger ones. He was still in his early teens. At least one of them was bought by I think it was Abraham Walkowitz, who paid twenty-five or thirty-five dollars for it. It must have taken his last cent.

Do you remember any of the other students in Chase's classes?

Robert Henri's classes. Because Henri had moved in there. He had come back from Paris. He was a younger man and had new ideas and became the leading teacher and spirit of the class there. In my class were George Bellows, Glen Coleman—oh, God, I've forgotten now.

Did you study with Chase himself?

At Shinnecock, that's all.

How did he teach his classes?

There was a big V-shaped board with racks. Students' paintings would be placed on one side, then turned around. The class gathered—a tremendous big class—and outsiders were welcome, too, and he would criticize the paintings brilliantly and interestingly. There was an episode I remember very well that I tell about in my autobiography. One time the screen was turned, and we all saw to our horror a dreadful bunch of black spheres, which seemed to mean nothing. I don't think they were abstractions, but they were certainly not realistic in any sense. And Chase took off his glasses, looked at them very carefully and said, "Who did these?" A woman way at the back, somebody we'd never seen before, piped up, "I did, Mr. Chase." Very politely, not being sarcastic or anything, he said, "Madam, I don't quite understand." And she said, "Well, I felt that way, Mr. Chase." He said, "Madam, the next time you feel that way, don't paint." He used to have a question box, and we'd put in serious questions, but every little while we put in this question just for the fun of hearing him answer it: "Mr. Chase, who do you think are the greatest American artists of today?" He would read that very seriously out loud and say, "Mr. Whistler, Mr. Sargent, and myself, if you like."

He was very dressy always. Beautiful, immaculate clothes; a fine cravat, always with a jeweled ring around it; a mustache and goatee—beard—always well groomed. When he painted for the class, he painted in his best clothes. He said there was no more excuse for an artist to get smeared with paint than for a surgeon to get himself smeared with blood. Quite often he painted for the class. And it was always interesting to us. He painted a great number of still lifes. At the Art Students League, which I never attended, they used to have exhibitions where they would make fun of different artists. Of Chase they'd have a still life of some sort with the slogan, "While there's still life, there's hope."

How did you decide on architecture?

Because my family, knowing that I loved art and was good at it, urged me strongly not to become an artist, because you could never support yourself by art. So architecture seemed the nearest allied profession that would promise me a living. Three years of that were enough to convince me that I didn't want to become an architect.

You had studied with Henri at his school in New York during the winters?

Most of my years at Columbia. After that I lived at home in Tarrytown at my mother's house, commuting every day to New York, and then going back, of course, at night, to the Henri School. I found the night classes to be the best, with the most earnest, hard-working people outside of art who managed to scrape together enough to pay for studying art at night. Eventually I quit Columbia, but still kept on commuting to New York to go to the Henri School. Then I graduated myself from that by going to Monhegan Island on the coast of Maine. There I found, of course, that I had to support myself at anything I could get. The only jobs in the summertime were working for summer cottagers around their places, including—and this was a plum when I could get it—emptying backhouses for five dollars each. It was a horrid job, but I'd wear rubber boots and shovel it out.

Then I built my own little two-room house. Put my study of architecture into practice and learned how to build. From there on I got jobs building for other people. Finally I built one, two, three, four, five houses on Monhegan Island. Two of them being the only houses on the place that were equipped with modern plumbing and all that kind of thing. My mother's house, which was the last I built, is still spoken of as the best-built house on Monhegan.

Did you study with Henri?

I studied with him, and half-days for one year with Kenneth Hayes Miller. But Henri was the most important teacher in the school in those days. And he remains one of the most important teachers of art that we've had in America. He had a great influence on people. I was never a devoted follower of Henri's, as Bellows, Guy Pène du Bois, Coleman, and others were.

Did you get to know some of those other people well?

Oh, yes. I used to see them every day. We organized a baseball team. I organized it, really, because I was the most active in things of that sort. We formed a little league—the Art Students League, the National Academy School, and the Henri school. I'm sure that in every single game we played we licked the hell out of the others. We had Bellows, who had played at Columbus, Ohio, on the University of Ohio baseball team and was, I think, good enough to have become a professional ballplayer if he had wanted to. Fortunately he didn't. But we had to have everybody play—Miller, even Coleman, who looked like something the cat had brought in. Not the physique of an athlete in any sense.

How did Henri conduct his classes?

You had a model posing. The students sat at work drawing or painting, and Henri walked from one to the other criticizing their work as it reflected or did not reflect the model before them.

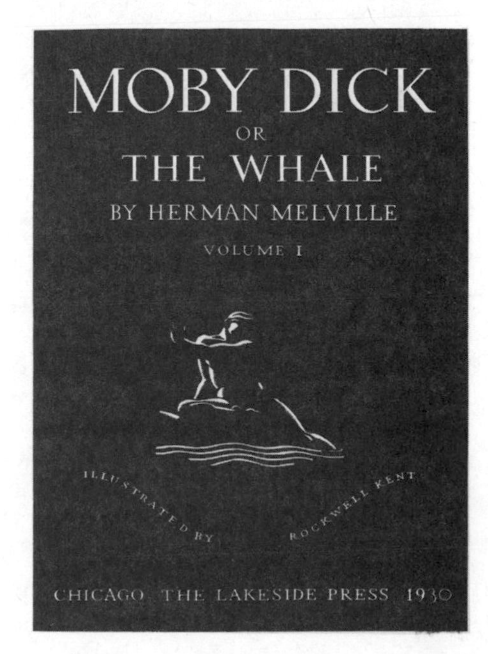

Rockwell Kent, title page for *Moby Dick*, by Herman Melville, published by The Lakeside Press, Chicago, 1930. (*Courtesy the Weyhe Gallery, New York*)

There was a joke we used to play on newcomers to the class. We had a middle-aged man in the class named Toft, I think. We had him appear on the first day that Henri was expected to criticize the new pupil. When Toft arrived the students would get up and say, "Good morning, Mr. Henri," and help him off with his coat. Then he'd walk up and down looking at things, and he'd pick up this new student's work and begin something like this: "Well, you, of course, have studied a great deal before, because..." "No, I never did, Mr. Henri." "Well, this is amazing! Students, I want you to come here and look at..." And we'd go on with that kind of thing. Then perhaps he'd turn from there to Edward Hopper—to a drawing by him (Hopper always drew beautifully)—and give him the devil, maybe even strike him. And the new student would come to Hopper's defense. Oh, we had lots of fun in that class.

Hopper was a very brilliant, Sargent-like painter. We students didn't particularly approve of him, but he was brilliant in that manner of painting. And then Goltz. And, let's see, Vachel Lindsay was a student—he never painted well. His real forte was his poetry.

What about Miller, who was also teaching there?

He had a separate class—a portrait class, not a life class, as I remember it. I painted under him a little bit.

One summer, through my artist aunt, who in her younger days had studied with Abbott Thayer—I got him to accept me as a sort of apprentice to help him in the method of working that he had adopted. He would carry a big painting to a certain point, where he would like to make some changes, but it was so good he didn't like to risk it. So he would have his apprentice make a copy of that unfinished painting, and it had to be a good copy, too. Then he would take the copy and go on with that, leaving the other one intact in case he wanted to go back to it. But while he was waiting to give me work of that sort, I had time to paint by myself. I painted landscapes, as I had been doing at Shinnecock. One day he saw what I was doing and said, "That's better than anything Chase ever did." It wasn't, but he said so. Anyhow, that pleased me tremendously. What pleased me more was that he said, "You're too good to waste your time working for me. I want you to paint for yourself. Do what you please."

What kinds of paintings and ideas interested you as a student in those days? Who were the older, established artists that you were interested in?

The main thing that interested me in those days, aside from earning a living (which I did not do through art, not for years and years, if ever), was working at common labor—carpentry, house-building. I worked as a lobsterman with a two-man dory. That was tremendously exciting to me. I loved it. It's had more influence on my whole life and way of thinking than anything I ever did, outside of painting itself—working on Monhegan and living among those people as one of them, getting to know working people instead of dilettantes like picture painters. This was more to me than anything else in my life.

What was so important about lobster fishing?

I was out on the sea. I recall when I first went there, it was just to paint pictures. I'd sit on the headland looking at the sea. Down below there would be men working in weltering seas, drawing these dories and pulling in their traps. And it came over me: My

God, what would people like myself be if people like that didn't do the work of the world for them? I got a real inferiority complex that I could only overcome by becoming a workman myself. Which I did—and as good as any of them. I don't mean as expert a lobsterman or anything like that, but I could row as well and as long as any other man. Well-drilling was another thing. Many wells I've drilled on Monhegan. It was drilling by hand. Swing an eight-pound sledge—two men, one holding the drill, turning it each time, and the other swinging. I could swing that sledge all day—an eight-hour day—day after day. It was marvelous. And it was wonderful to work with people and to feel that I was a workingman, because I'd come to have a disrespect for people who just painted pictures—onlookers on life, commentators on life. I was part of life itself. I loved hard work and what it was doing for me. There's more satisfaction in building a house than in painting a picture of one. Or even in planning it.

But architecture, in spite of my not having stayed at Columbia, was for years my mainstay for supporting my family and myself. Because I married at twenty-six, and my wife began having children. I couldn't support them by painting, because I never sold a picture. I was at Monhegan painting, and my aunt arranged with a dealer in New York named Clausen to hold the first exhibition of my work. It was a tremendous success critically, but no one bought a thing. I gave a picture to Henri, which he later very generously gave back to me because the Metropolitan Museum wanted a picture of mine. Then, needing money—my wife was quite sick after the birth of our second child and had to get out of the city for the summer—but how to get it? I was working in an architect's office, but earning very little. Davies told me to go and see William Macbeth. He said, "He's a very fine man. He teaches Sunday school and things of that sort." Now, Macbeth had already shown an interest in my pictures, so I went and told him my situation and that I had to have money. He said, "Well, how would five hundred dollars do?" I said that would be wonderful. I said, "All my paintings are stored in this or that warehouse. You go there and take what you think is the equivalent." He picked thirteen paintings, all of them with frames that had cost me forty or fifty dollars apiece. The paintings included that *Black Rock*, which is now in the Wadsworth Atheneum. I can't enumerate them all. Every one of them is now in an important museum and has brought some thousands of dollars each. But divide five hundred by thirteen and subtract from that thirteen times forty-five for the frames, and the pictures brought me less than a few dollars each.

What architectural firms did you work for?

Mostly for a firm called Ewing and Chappell. The firm was formed this way: through the death of an aunt my mother had inherited quite a little money and decided to build a house for us in Tarrytown. It was to be really a pretty fine house. To get an architect to design it, she naturally turned to me for suggestions. I knew a family called Ewing in Tarrytown. The older son was head draftsman for one of the good New York architectural firms—Carrère and Hastings. I talked with him, and he said he would love to do it and that he had been thinking of starting a firm of his own with a friend, who was also a Beaux-Arts student—George Chappell. They set up together and gave me my first job as a draftsman. I continued to work for them on and off for fifteen years, I think, until at last I got through with architecture. I was earning enough money for me and my family to go off in the country and paint somewhere, and I was always sure of a job, because I was good. I'm not boasting. It was about time I got to be good at something, and I was extremely good as an architectural draftsman. Good as a designer, and particularly useful at what is called rendering. I would take the scale drawings of a house, make a three-dimensional picture of it in perspective on watercolor paper, and then make that house as though it had been built, with trees and vines and flowers growing around it and people coming and going and so forth. And that was extra money I would make.

You were included in the Independents Show that Henri organized in 1910?

At the time of the first Independents Show, I was living on Caritas Island with J. G. Phelps Stokes, a wealthy man who was devoted to social work in the East Side slums in New York and had married a very fine young woman of East Side background. He had a little island you reached by a bridge from the mainland on Long Island Sound. That was at Stamford. I would commute from there to work in New York, and, as a refresher, I went to the Henri School again at night to draw from a life class. They had then moved uptown to the Lincoln Arcade Building. (Everyone said it was full of bedbugs, but I never happened to see one.) So I couldn't be active in the organization of the first Independents Show, though I had one or two pictures there. I *was* active in the organization of the second Independents Show at the Grand Central Palace.

What was the feeling about the National Academy? It was still the great influence.

Had been. I had fought it. The first and only time I sent to the National Academy—no, I sent once more. I sent two pictures, and both of them were sold—one to Smith College and one to a private individual—so I had no personal grievance against it. But I was all against its sentimental influence on American art at that time. And, in particular, against its attempt to grab a piece of Central Park for the erection of its building. I fought that, with others, and we were successful. Because it was outrageous. It's only a private club. It has no business in a public park. I've never showed at the National Academy since those days, except a few prints—wood engravings—at the insistence of John Taylor Arms, who said I had to become at least an associate member of the academy. And he railroaded it through without my consent or anything. So I was made an associate member as a printmaker. About a year and a half ago, I was asked by the academy to accept full membership, but I refused.

But weren't the painters that were involved with the Independents Show rebelling a great deal more against the academy and the very sweet traditional . . . ?

Looking back on it I realize that the younger painters had been strongly influenced by Henri and what was later called the "ashcan school," which didn't deserve a dirty name like that. It simply insisted on artists drawing their material from life itself, not sentimentalized life, but people as they actually were, especially the underprivileged classes. My own paintings there were not influenced, and I was never much influenced, by Henri, because I was a landscape painter, and at that time, I was painting out-of-doors.

What made you decide to go to Newfoundland?

Well, I decided that, though Monhegan was fine, a wonderful place, I wanted something more rugged, and from all I'd heard of Newfoundland that was the place to go. There I virtually rebuilt a tumbledown house, and the family came out from New York to join me. Then war broke out, and people decided that there was no such thing as a picture painter, that I was wandering around on hillsides not to paint pictures, but to make charts of the coast for the Germans. Anyhow, it got spread around that I was a German spy. Finally we were ordered to leave the country. Last summer in response to a wonderful invitation from the premier, my wife and I were invited there as guests. He wrote me saying that from papers that had come into his hands he'd learned all about the earlier case, and he wanted to atone for an injustice done me fifty years ago. We went in July, but stayed just a little over a week. We could have stayed indefinitely. It was a wonderful visit.

After I was fired out of Newfoundland, we lived for about a year on Staten Island. I was supporting myself largely by making illustrations for *Vanity Fair* and other things, and occasional little odd jobs, rendering, things of that sort. Then I decided to go to Alaska. I took my oldest son, who was eight, and we spent about a year there.

When did you start doing the illustrations for Vanity Fair*?*

I'd been doing that right along because the firm I worked for, Ewing and Chappell—George Chappell was wonderful. He wrote poetry—light verse, humorous verse. He would write the poem, and I would make the illustrations. They'd be published together in *Vanity Fair*. I didn't use my own name. The first drawing that I took to Frank Crowinshield, who was editor, was unsigned. He said, "Oh, you must sign it." I said, "I'm unwilling to put my name on my pictures." He said, "Put any name. How about Young Landseer?" "Oh," I said, "pick something better than that. How about Hogarth Junior?" So I became Hogarth

Junior. I illustrated for them for years. And also for *Puck*, *Harper's Weekly*, and other things.

Haven't you written about advertising art as opposed to say, fine art?

I may have exploded about advertising. I did a good deal of advertising work and was always hampered by it. The advertisers had the idea that the artist had *no* ideas. So they'd say, "Here's the idea. You draw it. You make a picture of it." I couldn't stand that kind of thing. The most successful advertising work I've done has been entirely out of my own head—no interference whatever from those Madison Avenue, quote, minds.

You like making beautiful books, don't you?

Yes. Because good printing, good bookmaking, good binding is as important in the field of literature as dressing well is important in society. Tremendously important. People may not realize it, but a thing has got to look nice, feel nice, and be nice.

Did you select the books, or did the publishers?

They were published by R. R. Donnelley and Sons, the Lakeside Press in Chicago. They're not publishers, but they're fine printers. They do everything from telephone directories to Sears Roebuck and Montgomery Ward catalogues to beautiful books. They wanted to publish some American classics, a selected few just to show what they could do in bookmaking. They proposed that I illustrate Richard Henry Dana's *Two Years Before The Mast*. I said, "Well, it's a book I'd like to do, but I'd prefer to do *Moby Dick*." They said, "All right, then you do *Moby Dick*." They expected a one-volume book. I started work on it, then wrote to them and said I wanted to do so many illustrations for this book that it must be two volumes. They said, "All right, we'll double the price, we'll pay you for two books." Then I worked on it some more. I wrote to them again and said it had to be three volumes. To my surprise, they said, "All right, then we'll pay you for three books." And that's the way *Moby Dick* was done. I had entire charge of everything in collaboration with their very fine typographer. The paper had to be of my choice, the type used, the designing of the cover, everything. The set had to be boxed. I got the idea of an aluminum box. They said, "Well, that's interesting. It's never been done. We'll get the figures on it." They reported back that the figures were too high; they couldn't afford it. So I decided on my own to write to Alcoa. I said, "Look here, this is a brand new field for the use of aluminum. It's never been done." And the figure I got from Alcoa was so low that the Lakeside Press promptly accepted it. They considered it the most beautiful book ever published in America. The only black title pages that ever were. And they were engraved by me on the metal.

Why did you go to Greenland?

Because I'd always been interested in Norse explorations and so

Geoffrey Clements

Rockwell Kent, *Cloud Shadows*, oil on canvas, 34" x 44", 1965. (*Courtesy Richard K. Larcada, New York*)

forth. I had intended to go to Iceland in 1916 and 17, but, because of the war, it was impossible. So I decided to go to Alaska. But I've always been interested in Iceland and have devoured their sagas, everything that I could get in translation. I was attracted to Greenland, not only because of its past history, but because of its icy mountains: "From Greenland's icy mountains,/From India's coral strand" [Bishop Reginald Heber, *Greenland's Icy Mountains*]. Well, I'm not the least bit interested in their "coral strands," but I do love the icy mountains. And I love the people there. I had a wonderful life in Greenland for two years.

All your travels seem to have been to very cold places. You've never gone much to the tropics, have you?

No, I don't like the tropics. I like cold weather. It doesn't bother me. I get cold, but I don't catch cold. You don't catch cold by being cold. In Alaska, every morning my young boy and I used to get out of bed, turn on the stove to get good and hot, and then run naked out of doors and roll in the snow. I've done that more or less until quite recently. It's not as cold as a cold bath.

You had a commission in 1930 with Jo Mielziner–a mural in the Cape Cod Playhouse.

Yes. That was a good job. It's a big ceiling thing. I didn't paint it actually. I made the cartoons for it, but very carefully. Then, in association with Mielziner, who does stage design and things like that, it was executed by professional scene painters. Now, at the time of the execution of Sacco and Vanzetti, I had a big exhibition of my work scheduled in Connecticut somewhere—or Massachusetts, rather—at some important gallery. In protest against their execution by the state of Massachusetts, I refused to *ever* have anything more to do with that state. So I withdrew my exhibition. That was effective as a protest. And, subsequently, when I got this Cape Cod mural and accepted it, I realized that I had said I would never do anything for Massachusetts. So I refused to take a cent for my share. Jo Mielziner got all the money that was paid for it. He earned it. And he wasn't under any such pledge as I felt myself to be. So I did it for nothing. And I'm glad I did it.

Have you ever designed anything for the theater?

I designed the costumes for a Soviet production of *Peter Grimes*, the opera. They used some of my costume designs, but not my scenic designs. That's all I've ever had to do with the stage.

Were you in Russia for the opening of your exhibition at the Pushkin Museum?

No. I was refused a passport because I wouldn't answer the sixty-four-dollar question. They had me go down to Washington for a hearing. A lawyer accompanied me. I didn't need him. But I had already taken court action on this subject, and my lawyer insisted on a lawyer coming with me and sitting at my side in case I wanted him. But they had a lawyer there. He had a copy of a book I'd written [*It's Me O Lord*, 1955] just chuck full of places marked. God, it was a silly business. "Mr. Kent, did you write this book?" "Yes." "All of it?" "Yes." He turns a page and reads a passage. "Did you write that, Mr. Kent?" "I told you I wrote the whole book! I must have written everything in it." It made no difference. He had to go through with the reading of every little passage. It was quite friendly. He was decent enough. And as I left, he left, too. I was taking an elevator down; he was going up. And he said, "You know, Mr. Kent, when you leave the building, you'll find waiting for you on the sidewalk a lot of men from the press with television cameras and so forth." "Hooray," I said, and I grabbed him, "Come down with me." "No, you don't!" He fled. Well, there was a crowd there of the press and cameras and so forth. But nothing much was said. In the meantime, court action had been going on with the National Emergency Civil Liberties Committee supporting me. Their lawyer was Leonard Boudin, a wonderful constitutional lawyer. We lost in the first court, went to the court of appeals, lost again, and then finally went to the Supreme Court. Sally [Kent] and I went down there to hear that argument. And they were not impressive, those fellows sitting behind a bar, some of them very slouchy. The most slouchy being Justice Felix Frankfurter. Every little while his head would pop up like a jack-in-the-box, and he'd hurl a malicious sounding question at Boudin. He was particularly horrid. Well, finally the hearing ended. Boudin was utterly despondent. He said, "Well, we've lost it, and I feel terrible about it." I said, "Lost it? You have not! You've won it." (I like to tell this.) He said, "How do you figure that?" And I counted off three justices from whom there would be no chance. I counted four whom we could count on—liberals. And he said, "Yes, and how about the fifth?" I said, "The fifth is Frankfurter." He said, "My God, are you crazy? Why do you pick Frankfurter?" I said, "He's too good a lawyer not to side with you." And Frankfurter did. We won the case five to four with Justice William Douglas writing a beautiful opinion about it. That was the most important action I've ever taken in my life—public action. It freed countless thousands of American people. Because, not only could none of the Communists be granted a passport, if they lied they would be subject to investigation and discovery and serious penalties. A very important case, generally called the *Kent-Briehl* case. A Los Angeles psychiatrist, Dr. Walter Briehl, had taken the same stand in regard to passport requirements. Well, that was an important case. And that way, anyhow, my name will be in history.

In What Is An American? [1936] *you mention reaching your majority and the Republicans sending a carriage so you could go and vote. You said that you were going to vote Socialist and that you were going to walk to the polls.*

I became a member of the Socialist Party when I was a young man of twenty. My first vote was for Eugene V. Debs. I was an active member of the Socialist Party for years, but I spent so much of my time abroad or out of reach that, finally, I just let it go.

All of this really goes back to your youth.

Oh, yes. I haven't changed in anything. I haven't grown more intelligent. In fact, I often warn young people against their elders, who are apt to say to them, "Well, when you get older, you'll know better." And I say, "You won't know better. The best thoughts you have are when you're young, and the best you can do is never to give up those thoughts." And that's the only thing that is notable about me—that I have not changed. All my best feelings came into being when I was young.

Geoffrey Clements

Thomas Hart Benton, *Self-Portrait*, December 24, 1934. TIME cover of Thomas Hart Benton. (*Reprinted by permission from TIME, The Weekly Newsmagazine; copyright Time, Inc., 1934*)

THOMAS HART BENTON

2

Son of a Missouri congressman, Thomas Hart Benton (1889–1975) became a figure of American folk legend during his lifetime. His first public recognition came when he was still a teenager, as a result of the cartoons he did for the *Joplin American*. In 1908, after studying briefly at the Art Institute of Chicago, he went to live and work for three years in Paris, where he discovered modern art, and where, in late 1909, he met Stanton Macdonald-Wright, who became a lifelong friend. Intelligent, but uncomfortable with aesthetes, Benton soon rejected the modernist tendencies he had so quickly espoused under Macdonald-Wright's influence. The response to his cartoonlike drawings of sailors, done while he was serving in the United States Navy during World War I, confirmed his embrace of popular cultural views. An example of an early abstractionist unable to fulfill his promise, Benton, like many of his generation, rejected the imaginative adventure of modernism. Seeking sustenance from the established traditions of mural painting, he attempted to create a historical continuity with the accomplishments of the old masters, a cultural misunderstanding that precipitated a compulsive, ritualistic technique-bound style. In 1919, the artist began to construct complicated three-dimensional Plasticine structures, based upon drawings and painted in colors, to serve as models for his murals and large paintings.

In the following interview, conducted on July 23 and 24, 1973 at Martha's Vineyard, Massachusetts, where he had summered since 1920, Benton implies that the island, not the Midwest, is the home of regionalism. He was fascinated by the bold contrasts in the New England character, so dramatically different, he felt, from that of the bland middle American he knew so well.

Throughout his life, Benton felt that Paris, not New York, represented art. Always hankering after grandeur, but unable to achieve an international reputation, he remained a painter of America's domestic scene and history.

As a teacher, Benton's supportive personality was crucial to his pupils, whether or not they agreed with the convoluted complexities of the art rituals he expounded. In the Fairfield Porter interview in this book, Benton is characterized by one of his most articulate students. It was left to his most famous student, Jackson Pollock, to transform Benton's anthology of attitudes into a methodology and ideology that became a crucial breakthrough for twentieth-century American art. Pollock's art offers insights into the American mind, life, and spirit far surpassing those of his teacher.

I realized that, while I could make pictures, there were a lot of things I didn't know, such as perspective and so forth. So I went to the Chicago Art Institute to learn. From there, through a fellow named Frederick Oswald, I got interested in painting—painting in watercolor—and in Japanese prints. Oswald was a lucky find for me. He gave me an idea of art. He saw my pen-and-ink stuff, which was newspaper-style stuff—crosshatching and all that. He showed me the pen-and-ink drawings of the Spanish illustrator Daniel Vierge—a very skillful kind of pen and ink. I copied those and shifted my pen-and-ink style—made it more realistic. And he got me to drawing directly from models, which I had never done before.

Did that change your attitude about drawing?

Oh yes, of course. I changed immediately. I'd been using imaginative stuff, and imaginative stuff is largely made up of what you've copied.

Did you have plaster-cast drawing in Chicago?

Yes. I was not very good at it. The trouble is that you put a kid on it and he doesn't know anything about icy cold. So after you've learned something.... Listen, I go all over Europe copying original sculptures, or have done so. I still do it a little. Good God, I was in Sicily a few years ago and made a lot of freehand copies.

What about the Art Institute in Chicago?

It was in that museum that I got my first interest, not from their possessions, but from exhibitions of Japanese prints. I learned from those prints that there was such a thing as controlled composition. They had two exhibitions; I saw only one. Because of James Whistler's influence, there was great interest in Japanese art during 1907, 1908, around there.

What is "controlled composition"?

You plan it before you start working on it. Figure it out, not in your head, but roughly, somehow or other. These were highly patterned things, and it was very good for me to be faced with that. Otherwise, with my instincts, I would have become just a pure illustrator. I knew nothing about European art—"classic art," I should call it. That's a bum word. But, let's say, fifteenth-, sixteenth-, seventeenth-century art—I knew nothing whatever about it until I went to France in late August [1908]. I enrolled in the Académie Julian in Paris in September.

Why did you choose that academy?

That's what Oswald and what everybody recommended. We had no facilities in Chicago at that time for taking examinations for the Beaux-Arts. They did in New York. The rest of us in America just went to the Académie Julian. That's the only place you could go.

What was the academy like in 1908?

I registered at the beginning of classes in late September 1908. I was there until the late spring of 1909. Then I quit the place under the influence of a fellow named John Carlock, who said I could learn more drawing if I'd go to the Louvre and copy drawings there. And I think he was right.

Did you receive criticism at the academy?

I studied in the drawing classes of Jean Paul Laurens, who was then famous in France. He was a historical painter. I should have had some affinity for him, but I didn't, of course. He never looked. He just walked around the class. He had a stooge, one of his students, who did all the criticism. It was standard academic drawing. And it's a bore. The model stayed there for two weeks. You got tired of looking at it. Well, I tell you, they introduced me—they taught me skills of doing that kind of thing. I was never very good at it. But take Leon Kroll and Max Weber—they were expert at it. They were there the same time I was. They were both at the Beaux-Arts, so I didn't see much of them.

In those early decades so many Americans went to Paris and stayed.

I wanted to stay, but I had to go away. Everybody else wanted to stay.

Why?

It looked like you got used to that life. And, what the hell, you felt there wasn't any art in America. So the hell with it. You wanted to stay because you were living in a world of art, not a life, not a cultural life. You were just living in a highly elitist society. It was poor, but it was elitist.

Did you meet any French painters?

Oh, yes. I knew a lot of them, but none that amounted to a damn. I didn't know anybody who afterwards became important. I met Paul Signac once. And imitated him. As a matter of fact, I followed his pointillism for about a year. But though I made no close acquaintances, I made enough to be pretty much involved in the theoretic life of the time. Let's see, I knew André Lhote. Also Frederic Frieseke. Then there were Americans like Morgan Russell, Arthur Lee, Stan Wright (Stanton Macdonald-Wright), who was my age—actually he was much younger. He and Morgan later founded what they called synchromism.

How did you meet them?

In the cafés. In the Café du Dôme. That's where everybody went. So I went, too.

Did you visit other artists' studios?

No, it was largely café life. There was a certain kind of curious secrecy with all the damned artists. They didn't want to show you what they did.

I studied privately for a while with a French painter named Berenol, whose forebears had been Indochinese colonists. He was a nut on oriental coloration, on theories of oriental color, which was quite different from Signac, who was interested in spectral colors—scientific—[Michel Eugène] Chevreul and all that damn stuff.

Did you read all those books on color theory?

Sure! Listen, there were no movies, there was no radio, there wasn't anything. So what did you do? You read. And of course they got cockeyed theories in their heads. What they read they couldn't understand. But they made it up anyhow. I was like all the rest of them. Paris between 1908 and 1911 was the most voluble world that you ever saw on earth. When you'd go into the Café du Dôme you couldn't hear anything for people arguing.

Did you hear much about cubism?

No. That's a very difficult question that's been thrown at me many times: that I must have been influenced by the cubists because they found a lot of cubist drawings of mine. But those were all done after 1919, and they're based on the drawings of Cambiaso, the sixteenth-century Italian cubist. I had no interest in Parisian cubism. I saw some of it, maybe the very earliest of, say, Juan Gris and Pablo Picasso's very early pictures of the Spanish style. I didn't get interested in cubism until 1919, when it was a dead issue. Well, not a dead issue, but it had done its thing by that time. What I was interested in was the three-dimensional world and trying to learn how to construct it.

What did you copy at the Louvre?

I never copied anything. I made sketches. Rough figures. The first thing I did was Titian's *Entombment*. You'd just hold a pad in your hand and make copies, rough copies, trying to see what you could find out. I was pushed into that by that fellow Carlock, who was a very interesting American in Montparnasse.

Was it difficult to meet French artists, or did you associate mostly with Americans?

No, I never got in with the Americans. There was a barrier set up by the older ones. Those who had been there a little earlier never welcomed the new ones. I associated with French people, until I met Carlock. Until I met Stanton Wright, I had no American companion in France—no English-speaking companion. And of course he had a lot of money and was able to take care of everything. So we got to going around. And he was lonely. We were about in the same age group. We got to be friendly. I met Morgan Russell through him. Morgan was ten years older than we were.

What about Macdonald-Wright's and Russell's synchromism?

I never knew anything about that. That was after I had left France. It hadn't come up then at all.

Why did you leave France in 1911?

I didn't have any money. I had to come back. I knew damn well I couldn't make a living in France. I thought I was going to be a portrait painter then. I went back to the Académie Julian style of portraits and started to practice that. I made a few. I went back to my hometown. Stayed there about seven months. I practiced this portrait business, and convinced my father that if I went to New York I could probably put this thing into use. I could make a good likeness. Well, I got there and couldn't. I went there in 1912, settled myself in the old Lincoln Arcade Building at Sixty-fifth Street and Broadway. One of the first persons I ran into in New York was Sam Halpert. I had known him—met him, seen him at the Dôme in Paris—but never really knew him. I thought I could find some way of making a living. I did get a few minor commercial jobs. Also I ran into a fellow named Ralph Barton, who was from Kansas City. As a matter of fact, my uncle had killed his great-grandfather in a duel in Missouri. We got acquainted and liked each other. He had worked on the *Kansas City Star* as a newspaperman, as I had. But he had gone into commercial art and had had some success. He got me two or three small jobs, but generally I had a rough time. I stayed from June 1912 until late that autumn. Then my father thought I had better go back to our hometown. So I went. That's the reason I missed the Armory Show. I didn't come back to New York until June 1913.

What about people like John Sloan and...

I didn't know them at that time. Later, from 1913, 1914, 1915, I met them—Robert Henri, Sloan, George Bellows, and all those. I met Rex Ingram—he had come out of Yale—and roomed with him. We both—everybody was short of money. Rex and I shared one of the rooms at the Lincoln Arcade. He came during the day and worked at sculpture. But in the meantime he had been an amateur actor and had gone into the movie business, so he abandoned sculpture and became a director. I believe it was in 1914 that I first began to work for the movies as a set designer and general worker. By 1914 Rex was associate director with Gordon Edwards, a rather famous director. Anyhow, for friendship's sake, he got me a job. I was hired like any old scene painter. They did a lot of romantic stuff in the movies—silent movies, all in black and white. I used to go down to the public library and draw an Irish castle, or some goddamned thing like that, and then make a black-and-white thing that was used as a backdrop for the scene. It was done boldly enough so it looked like something real behind the actors. I did that off and on until 1917.

I moved to Fort Lee then. And there I met Walt Kuhn and Arthur B. Davies, "Pop" [George] Hart, and other artists who also lived around Fort Lee and the Palisades. The real truth of how I met the artists was that in 1914 Stan Wright and Morgan Russell brought their synchromist things back to New York. Now I knew Willard Wright, Stan's brother, and had run around with that crowd—George Nathan, Willard Wright, H. L. Mencken, and some other writers, no artists. When Stan brought those synchromist things back to New York, he had an exhibition. We had a hell of a time finding a place to show them. There were no galleries. Some woman had established one on Forty-fifth Street. She called it the Carroll Galleries. Wright had to pay for it. He hired the gallery, and they put synchromism in there. I used to go around there every day. After all, this was part of the smell of Paris, and I was interested. I began to meet artists there. Quite a number of them came in. It never got any réclame at all, or much attention, but a lot of artists came in to see that exhibition. So I would hang around, and I met them. At the same time I met John Weichsel of the People's Art Guild, I think through Sam Halpert, who also came to that show. None of the artists liked the show. It was rather brash; the whole damn thing was crude and had a lot of effrontery. But anyhow, I began to meet artists.

I had not lived in an art world in New York before the synchromists brought their things there. I didn't do anything with it at the tme. It was two years later, when Stanton came back to New York—and I don't mind in the least saying it today—that I had a chance to exhibit if I made some synchromist paintings. So I made them. Well, it wasn't altogether that, but that was part of it. And, of course, that was what they spread around New York about me. And it was partly true. But I was interested also. I had already done—what do you call it? Spectral painting, under the influence of Paul Signac. But I had never monkeyed with it on large planes or with the idea of using it compositionally. I used it impressionistically. I was interested; it wasn't just a venal thing at all. Then I got my first attention, because the pictures I put in there raised a lot of stench. The newspaper men, by accident, picked them up. So I probably got more attention in the press in that Forum Show than almost anybody else.

The paintings you had in that exhibition were of large figures, weren't they?

That's right. But they were all spectral. I simply did Renaissance compositions with spectral color. That's all it was. But it looked strange at the time. I did exactly what you see in those drawings of Jack Pollock's, only with bright color. Henry McBride called them "quotations from the old masters." And that's what they were.

After the Forum Show, I continued that kind of exploration of Renaissance form. But I abandoned color and did them all in monochrome.

Thomas Hart Benton, *Poker Night–From a Streetcar Named Desire*, tempera and oil on panel, 36″ x 48″, 1948. Collection of The Whitney Museum of American Art, New York. Promised gift of Mrs. Percy Uris.

Why did you abandon color?

Because the problem of form interested me more than that of color. I worked on form for a year or so with very little color—all grayed gray. There was color there, but not very much. And really, *Still Life* is as near anything that I've got of what you might call a synchromist use of color—a vase of flowers, a banana, a couple of pieces of apple or something, split up. Most of these synchromist things I did—of course, I was foolish, but running out of canvas, I'd simply paint over them. When I'd change my style, I'd paint something else on them. I kept doing that for years. Then finally I'd turn the canvas over and paint on the back. We didn't care about it. We didn't work for money.

Your experience in the navy during World War I seems to have been very important as far as finding out who you were for yourself and to the world.

Yes. It was crucial. I think you've just about said it right. It threw me back on the kind of people that I'd been raised with—just ordinary boys, young men not of the art world. Also, through the obligations or duties I had, it threw me back on a highly objective work—I mean the world that was in existence outside of me, which I hadn't paid any attention to since I went to Paris. The ordinary world outside of the art world. That did have its effect, there's no question about it. No doubt something else would have forced me back onto that eventually, anyhow, because I was getting tired of just being an artist. I was bored with it.

Nothing was happening?

No. There was nothing to it. All you'd do was go down to Alfred Stieglitz's and argue with a lot of people. There just seemed nothing to it for me. Stan Wright said, when he left New York in 1918, "I'm tired of chasing art up the back alleys of New York. I'm going to get out of here." People all felt that way.

What about the older artists of that period?

They had a life. Sloan, Bellows, Henri, William Glackens—they had already been in touch with American life. They still kept the touch. You see, we people who were represented in the Forum Show were expatriates who had come back thinking we were above those people. In fact, we scorned them as old hat, no good. But at least they had some attachments. I didn't. None of us did.

The whole truth is that the spirit of the modern movement as an expression of the personality of the artist had not penetrated me at that time. I was thinking of art. This was also true of other of the synchromists—there were two at least. We were not thinking of art as an expression of our personality; we were thinking of making pictures. Quite a different kind of thing. But the only trouble with us was that we were making the pictures out of other pictures. Looking for form and looking for ways of doing it. so the navy had a terrific influence on me, threw me into a world where I stopped making pictures out of pictures entirely. You always make pictures out of pictures if you're an artist. You can't help it.

Your craft is there. You learn it from your predecessors. Now, there is no art born purely of a spontaneous response to nature except Grandma Moses's. But even that's made of other pictures that she'd seen before—good and amateurishly, but that's it.

What happened after the navy?

Back in New York I had a highly publicized exhibition of watercolors that I had made in the navy. This was at Charlie Daniels' gallery. Sold a few. Didn't get anywhere with it much. That was in 1919. I worked as a stevedore along the docks for several months. I got together enough money and got a place over on the East River. I worked there, still on form problems. I knew Rita [Piacenza Benton] then. She and a schoolteacher friend came up to this island [Martha's Vineyard] and found out that I could rent a barn. Old Tom Craven was then a—he wasn't an art critic—he wrote, and he taught English and Latin in high schools and private schools. He and I lived together. We decided to come up here and rent the barn that Rita told us about. I did my first regionalist pictures here, portraits of some of the people on the island.

Where did you meet Craven?

He was from Kansas. He was a writer and a poet. I met him in 1912 in New York. And he, like me, had come to New York to take it by storm. Didn't do it. He'd go back and teach in those damn schools. In the summer he'd come to New York. We'd frequently live together or in adjoining apartments. He was a good cook. He'd cook, and I'd wash the dishes. They used to think we were a couple of homosexuals because we were always together. But it was for the convenience. I've always liked the association of males, anyhow. Craven had very little interest in the arts until about 1919, though he had been sent to Europe and had done the regular tour like an Englishman. And being a methodical man, he had made notes on the galleries. Of course, he'd read John Ruskin, so he wasn't ignorant. But he was not prepared to be an art critic. In 1919 Scofield Thayer, who was interested in Craven's sonnets, was then establishing *Dial* magazine. He asked Craven to write an article on some art subject. Craven and I concocted it, and he put it into English and sold it to the *Dial*. Every time there was an art thing, Scofield would give it to him to do. And Craven became an art critic. Then, when the regionalist movement came on, he backed it, maybe overstrongly. That is he got—of course, he and Alfred Stieglitz didn't get along. And he would take cracks at the Stieglitz modern views once in a while.

Was it personal?

Yes. That's the way it began, anyhow. On the surface they got along. I never got along with Stieglitz either. Not at all. But we made a surface agreement. I thought he was a pain in the neck. He talked all the time; you never could get a word in. I like to talk a little myself. Listen, I don't think anybody alive ever really knew Stieglitz. He became kind of a legend. And he had a curious effect over a lot of the intellectuals. But Stieglitz was no intellectual. He knew nothing whatever about the background of painting or of anything that he showed. He was a hell of a photographer in a way.

How was he able to exert such influence?

He had a terrific ego, a great sense of self-projection. And he kept at it. But he was a strange guy, because his devotion to some of those artists, like John Marin, Marsden Hartley—Marin, mainly—was a true devotion. And just through association, or, say, exposure to art, I think he became in a way sensitive to certain aspects of it. For instance, he thought that all this stuff I was doing was pure academic, the kind of stuff that Pollock did. Which I did also before that—exploration of form. But some of the guys from Europe that he most supported did the same thing. It was all right for them to do it, but not for me.

How did you come to teach at the Art Students League?

As I say, I got to painting New England. There was a group up here from Harvard—liberals—that bought a place over on the South Shore, an old farm of several hundred acres. They turned it into a kind of intellectual resort. One of the leaders there was Stanley King, a liberal, who had made a fortune in leather goods during World War I. And there were such people as Felix Frankfurter, Jerome Frank, Roger Baldwin, Bernard De Voto.

And also there was Mike [Boardman] Robinson, who had come back from being a cartoonist on the London *Times*. He had just started to paint. Well, I knew more about painting than Mike did, and we got along all right. He was a hell of a draftsman. By 1926, Mike had sufficient power to get me a job at the Art Students League in New York. And I made it work. A hundred and three dollars a month. Our rent was forty-five dollars a month. So we had a basic living.

Did you have many students?

No. I began with very few, and never had a very big class. But I had some interesting people. I would say an awful lot of artists who became well known were my students there.

What did you teach the young art student?

What I taught was what I knew. I taught what I was trying to learn—better put it that way. I worked in the class. I had a model there. Ordinarily I didn't have a model. I drew there, too. We made compositional analyses. I started historical teaching—the way pictures had been made in the past. I had a semicubist and analytical process, which I first designed for Albert Barnes for his book. We quarreled, of course, and it was never done.

Analysis of pictures—cubist analysis—shows what their structure was. And when it came to impressionism and Barnes asked me, I said, "That's kind of difficult. There isn't much form there." Well, he got madder than hell at that. He was collecting some of these impressionistic paintings. It was an unpolitic statement. I published the articles I did for Barnes in *Arts* magazine in 1926 and 1927.

By the time I began to teach at the league the—what do you say?—the "return to the culture" had had enough impact. You see, you already had the writers—Sinclair Lewis, even Mencken himself, Theodore Dreiser, Sherwood Anderson—making an impact. When I began the regional stuff right here on this island, it got attention. You'd have to go back to the literature of the period to find out where and how it got attention. If there were any blacks down South who had talent and if they could raise the money, they'd send them to me.

Why was that?

Well, I was painting the South, too. Later they all turned against me terribly. They thought I was caricaturing the Negroes. That was after the Marxists got in. But up to 1928, I was all right with them.

Do you think there's a great deal that a teacher can give an art student?

I thought I could give. And some of them got a lot out of it. Even Jack Pollock. Now, I don't say I made him, by any means, but if he had had no formal basis for that damn stuff, if he hadn't gone through my class, what the hell would he have done? And Ed Laning is another case. Of course, he's more academic. But what would he have done if he hadn't had some formal training?

You've used the term "regional" a few times. When was it first used?

In the thirties, actually 1934. It was adopted from the regionalist group at Vanderbilt University in Nashville, Tennessee. Some Southern writers revolted against the effects of the cities and were going to write according to their region.

You mean Allan Tate and his group?

Yes. They were called regionalists. And that was transferred to fellows like Sinclair Lewis. So when we came onto the scene, when Grant Wood and John Curry and I had our first exhibition at Fred Price's old place—this was around 1934—we were dubbed regionalists. We didn't do it. But it's fairly accurate, descriptive. We were responding to the cultural situation around us, rather than just making pictures out of pictures.

Did the term have to do with the subject matter, or with the style of painting?

Oh, it had nothing to do with the style of painting. It was the subject matter of painting or what was stimulating—what was motivating you. But the form is—look, between Grant Wood, John Curry, and myself, the form is totally different. In fact, I was the only classicist among them, the only true academician. I'm a better academician than any of them. I know more about it even than Jean Paul Laurens, who was the great one.

You had a plan in the twenties to paint murals of the history of America.

They were formal experiments. I was also trying to find a meaning—a social meaning, a cultural meaning, one attached to the United States. I had that kind of background. I had done subject painting as a boy. I never did anything unless I had a subject. I didn't draw still lifes or flowers or things like that. It had to be Custer killing Indians, or Indians killing Custer, or the blowing up of the battleship *Maine*, and so on, or I wasn't interested. I never did anything without a subject. So I just went back to it. Psychologically this is where that return to the association of the common American type in the navy had a lot to do with my life, in throwing me right back to where I started. It got me out of an aesthetic world into another world, the world that I . . . In my youth I never thought of pictures as an aesthetic expression. They were pictures of *something*.

And I told you that, when I was in Chicago, the Japanese prints aroused a purely aesthetic interest. That was a combination of the two. But finally the aesthetic interests were—I got lost in them. Then the navy experience threw me back into another kind of world. I don't think I've lost my interest in the aesthetic properties of objects. As a matter of fact, purely aesthetic properties of objects have been extremely rare in the history of art. They've never been made for that.

How did you start making three-dimensional models for paintings?

Reading Tintoretto's models. They were very common in the High Renaissance. In fact, in a museum in Bologna, there is a document—a letter from an artist commissioning a sculptor to make a model according to certain specifications. He sent the drawings and everything.

You started making these quite early then?

No, not until 1919. I'd done some sculpture before, yes, but I had never thought of making models for paintings.

Do any of them exist for older works?

No. Some of them are big things. I made one twelve feet long for the mural in the state capitol building of Missouri. And the one for the Truman library was very carefully made and given to a guy to cast. He didn't know what he was doing and ruined it. The last one I made for the Joplin mural. The only models in existence from the Renaissance artists are fragments of those that El Greco made at his house in Toledo. Now, I never saw those. I tried to see them, but I couldn't make the guide understand French, or else he didn't want to bother with me.

How should one view the models?

You've got to stand in one place. All of them have got to be in certain positions. When you get to the side of it it's nothing.

Thomas Hart Benton, model for *Turn of the Century Joplin*, plasteline and wax, 12″ x 27″, 1971. Location unknown.

So they should be viewed looking down and from the center?
Yes. And if you put it up on the wall it would look like it's falling off. That was true of the figures. So it isn't good for a damn. So I never did keep them. A lot of my students make them. Jack Pollock made them when he was doing his early drawings.

Do you make a model for every painting?
For anything that's complex made from drawings.

The drawings come first, then you make a model?
Yes.

Then you color?
No. After I determine what the color scheme is going to be, I'll paint. And then, of course, you can't paint them like they are. It isn't nature. But a model shows you both color and form, and your memory—the planes sort of do the work for you.

Have you always made sculpture at the same time as the paintings?
Yes. I began sculpting even in Paris.

But you've never shown a great deal of it.
No. There's not too much left around. The head of Rita was made in 1918. That was just in plaster up until a few years ago, when we cast it. I never bothered with them. I do them to learn something. They help me paint. Or I think they do.

How do you decide what colors to use in the paintings?
I keep trying them out. Color, since I came to look upon it, was not used for itself, but to enhance or bring out form. Form finally came to mean almost sculptural form. In fact it's been that way all my life, to some extent. Even before I thought of sculpture, I modeled the things I made. Color was used to bring out form, not for itself. How do I determine the color? Well, of course, there's the subject—nature itself. If you've got a red tulip, you've got a red tulip to deal with. But you don't want red all by itself in the picture; you've got to distribute it. That's my idea of color as form. Color is part of the form when it's so distributed that you find it

repeated all over the picture. So I hunt on a relatively flat picture, merely hunting for some spacing of blocks of color so that red isn't only on one side of the picture. Now, today, some of the young artists paint pictures with red on one side and blue on the other. From my point of view that's no form at all; that's two different forms, considering color as a form. I try to distribute colors or tones of the same color over the picture. If there's pink going into the sky, well, of course, there's bound to be pink in the lower part of that landscape, where the sun hits the sand and gravel. Some people say, "Why the hell do you use color at all, if you're only using it as chiaroscuro or form?" Well, simply because the color brings it out in a way that you couldn't possibly get out of black and white.

Do you work through all these stages–making drawings from nature, then a three-dimensional model, then small studies, and then large studies?

And then the final painting. I never touch the final painting until I know what I'm going to do.

So there will be a small study, almost a miniature of...

Of nearly every painting I've made. That is, of paintings of any consequence.

I first made sculptural pictures, I mean small sculptures—well, I won't say, "first made them"—but I began making small sculptures shortly after my synchromist experience, in order to give more impact or reality to abstractions. I found out that the still lifes I painted direct from objects had more impact than the abstractions I made from my imagination. So I began making sculptures—constructions. I made them out of wire, paper, cloth—all kinds of things. This was before construction became an art in itself. I did it to improve an abstract painting, to give it more impact, to make it seem real. There are a few of those surviving. It was after that that I went into using them for representational pictures. Quite a number were made in 1917. I did a lot of paintings from them. The great trouble was that I was a little under the influence of Preston Dickinson then. He painted on charcoal paper all the time. A lot of them didn't last—they fell to pieces. Preston and I were very good friends, and when I saw him work at it I followed the practice. It was the cheapest way of doing it; canvas was expensive. So nearly all of my abstractions were made on paper. Later constructions were made for themselves. I've never felt that constructions were works of art. I'd make them and paint them a little different size.

So you were really making a model to paint?
Yes, that's right.

Do you find that you work out many of your painting problems . . . ?
Just the big form problems. And it also gives you light and shade. Though I sometimes shift the model to control that light and shade. The handling of them is quite flexible. If you were to copy them it would be a copy of the model—it wouldn't look like nature at all. In addition, I generally make a watercolor on the spot.

You mentioned your murals and your interest in mural technique. What was it that interested you in murals before you had made them?
The first paintings I ever noticed in my life were the murals in the Library of Congress, as a seven-, eight-year-old boy. I went to the library frequently. I would say, and this is just guesswork, that they must have made me want to do that. Because by the time I really got into painting in Chicago—I was a draftsman most of the time—I wasn't thinking of murals. But in France you saw so much of it. I remember the Salon Carŕe and the great Rubens room and *The Apotheosis of Catherine de Medici*. I'm sure I wanted right away to paint a great big wall like that. But I didn't begin this large-scale painting until 1919. That was for the Epic of America historical set. Only two sets were ever finished because of the physical business of taking care of them. I couldn't do it; so I had to abandon it. And right after that came the New School mural. I had a wall. I did it for nothing. And the Whitney Museum mural. That was done for nothing, too. Then the Indiana mural, for which I got ten thousand dollars, which was good money, but, mind you, that was two hundred feet long and twelve feet high.

Do you make a large drawing in sections?
I make very careful studies, then I square them up onto a larger

scale. By that time I know the actions of the figures. Then I make drawings of the figures. Then they are put into the enlarged drawing and the whole thing is scaled up onto the wall. Sometimes these scalings come down to one-sixteenth of an inch. I've been very lucky in having draftsmen help me. I had a very good draftsman with the Missouri mural. He was a great help in getting the thing enlarged. And I had pretty good helpers with the Truman Library mural. I never let any artist paint on the mural. I do all that myself. I'm pretty fast when I know what I want to do. For instance, I may take weeks preparing some damn thing—well, I won't say weeks, but days and days—but when I paint it, I'll probably do it in a day.

What do you do on a mural if you run into a problem?

I never change it. I've learned too well from my early experiences with changes that the minute you make a change it offers problems all over again. So once I've made up my mind, I don't change anything at all. Everything I put in murals is drawn from nature. The organizational problem there is quite terrific. Things in nature are not like you want them.

You have to work to get things into a position in an organization. That's my definition of form. I can't explain that. That doesn't seem to be understood today. The form to me is always something that is so organized that the parts are all coordinated. And this is the way I taught. You asked me yesterday why I taught the kind of drawing you saw by Pollock, which is a paraphrase of Renaissance, Greek, and other paintings and sculptures. The idea is to find how to make a form, coordinate these parts. So when you get a fellow like Mark Rothko, who makes a flat thing with a lot of different colors in it—well, I don't call it form. It might be a color experiment. I make those myself sometimes just to see what subtleties I can get with color itself. All of Pollock's things, at least in the beginning, started out to be some kind of form. And there remains form in all of them. All the peripheries are never completed. You could always keep on going in any direction with any one of them. But that's partly true even of the best organized composition. You can always find a hole in it. So when you stop form-making, it's nearly always arbitrary. But in Pollock's case it was extraordinarily arbitrary. He just quit when the canvas ran out.

It's interesting to compare the drawings he did as a student and then to see what happened as he developed. He kept those same moving rhythms.

The same rhythms. Now mind you, I don't make any claim to have affected Jack Pollock very much. He learned those rhythms out of the Renaissance, where I learned them. So I had nothing to do with it, except that I guided him in that direction in the early part of his life. That's the only thing. People make too much of the influence I had over him. The only influence was the stuff that I directed him to. And I was as much influenced by them as he was. Even though I make a picture of some American scene and am supposed to be what they call an "American scene" painter, there's the classic design even in one of those things.

I just like human beings in their old life, maybe because it's associated with the fun of living during my youth. And that was part of it. That was it. There weren't any automobiles. I was not raised in an industrial center. I liked steam engines because their movements were presented to the eye very clearly. The pistons and wheels on a steam engine are fascinating to watch. I used to watch them by the hour. But in the highly industrialized world we live in now, most of the mechanical power is disguised so there's no more interest in it. You don't see it in action.

Were you interested in traveling? Did you look for subjects?

To paint. And adventure. To do things. Adventure. And then for subject matter for drawings. I like to do it. I'm not as fast as I used to be, but I still draw all the time. I could do those drawings very rapidly during my best period—the twenties and early thirties. They're pencil, pen-and-ink wash. I did them first in pencil. But I carried a knapsack on my back with the things in it, and they began to rub. So every night I'd put pen and ink over them. Then a wash, a light wash to keep the pencil lines so they didn't rub. I developed that technique through necessity. It became a regular formula.

The wash always looks as if it had been put on separately.

It is. It's to keep the pencil lines. At least *I* can see the pencil lines, whether you can or not. Maybe to people it doesn't look good.

The light in your paintings is extraordinary. Is it from models?

It *is* extraordinary. You never quite see it in nature. All the vibrancy is in the painting itself. The light comes from the play of color all around.

So the models are more important than one might assume.

Yes, sure. They determine the light and shade a good deal and the concentrated—one reason you make them is you concentrate the form. You see, I can make a picture up without ever making a model. And I did hundreds of them before I did this. But it doesn't have the same impact.

Ivan Albright, *Self-Portrait at 55 East Division Street*, lithograph on paper, 16⅞″x 13⅛″, 1947. Collection of The Whitney Museum of American Art, New York. Gift of Mr. and Mrs. Sylvan Cole, Jr.

IVAN ALBRIGHT

3

A son of the painter Adam Emory Albright, student of and later monitor for Thomas Eakins, Ivan Albright (b. 1897) began modeling as a child for his father. Both he and his twin brother, Malvin Marr, who signs his paintings Zisissly, began drawing at about the age of seven. Because he lacked an aptitude for mathematics, Albright's first ambition, to be an architect, foundered. It was only after service in World War I that he went to art school, first studying at the Art Institute of Chicago School under Leopold Seyffert, then at the Pennsylvania Academy of the Fine Arts and the National Academy. For years, to maintain a state of purity untainted by commerce, the artist withheld his works from the marketplace, supporting himself by designing and building houses.

Essentially a still-life painter, Albright invests considerable preparation in the motif of each work. An aversion to newness as a quality has led him to use materials touched either by life or with historical significance. Once the elements have been gathered, he assembles the motif. Preferring to work with natural northern light, he has established a complex procedure to ascertain the best angle from which to observe the subject while painting. As he explains in this interview, which was conducted on February 5 and 6, 1972, at his studio in Woodstock, Vermont, an object can be painted from many viewpoints. His easel is equipped with a universal joint, which allows the canvas to be tilted and turned, affording a controlled application of brush strokes in different directions. To be able to work from many viewpoints, he prepares a chart of the location of the motif in relation to the easel and catalogues the position from which he will view it, marking the relationship of his overall view of the subject to the specific view from which he will then paint. This complex early-planning stage contributes to the intensity contained in and generated by Albright's works. Color is applied just once, because, as the artist says, "With a complicated program such as this, you don't want to make changes once the actual painting has started."

Infusing the tradition of the well-made painting with high moral standards, considerable technical skill, and a volatile imagination, Albright has produced some of the most provocative paintings in recent time. He is among those few most important contributors to our culture: the mavericks.

Would you start with some family background?

I was born a twin, an identical twin. My dad, Adam Emory Albright, was an artist. He painted children. At the age of about two months, I began posing for him, then my brother and I both posed for him from about the age of six to about twelve. We started drawing, I think, at the age of six or seven.

Did you start drawing by yourself?

Well, no. We were very silly. We even had a model; we'd hire a model for a little bit and draw in charcoal for an hour a day. We should have started drawing casts. Until I was about twenty-one, until World War I, I was drawing every summer.

Were these formal classes with your father?

No, no, my dad didn't teach us. At least he didn't say anything. Which was good. And I didn't know anything. We used to go to the Chicago Art Institute from the time I was three or four on, so I was acquainted mostly with American artists. By the time I became an artist there wasn't anything to it. It was the same as if I were a butcher. There was no glamour to it at all.

I started going to art school. I went to the Chicago Art Institute school for four years, then to the Pennsylvania Academy, and later to the National Academy. That was for Charles Hawthorne. George Bellows was in Europe. The only one I wanted was Bellows or Hawthorne. I preferred Bellows at the time.

What was the Chicago Art Institute school like? Who did you study with?

Who I studied with didn't amount to anything. I was free. I started right out painting. I didn't go through the drawing part; I thought I knew it. I was monitor in two or three classes. The institute was all right. I think it was in my third or fourth year that I started to try to think for myself. I didn't listen to anyone much. Finally I started to analyze and take notes. I was trying to think what I was going for. I was going for form. In those days everything was color; they didn't know what form was. I kept asking, and they'd say, "You don't know what you're talking about. Why don't you just copy the model." But I wouldn't go for that.

What kind of color?

Color, for instance, without any relationship to anything. What I mean is that they didn't know. Say I'm talking about a model. First there's a body, then there's light on that body, and then there's individual color on the body. But they were confusing the form of the body and the color of the body and the light on the body all together.

By the time I got out, I was on the way to thinking of studying, of thinking outside of making a picture. Then I went to the Pennsylvania Academy. It had a fairly good bunch of teachers like Daniel Garber, Charles Grafly, and others. I should mention that in Chicago I took up heads under Albin Polasek, the sculptor.

If you're making a stone sculpture, you stop because you can't go into it. If you're making something that's fleshy, a woman or a man, your finger can sink in like it can sink into a pillow. Then you get gradations of shading and modeling. And all that a shadow is is the opposite side without the light hitting it. But it's underneath; you've got to make the form underneath, and then you want to shade on top. You go through it delicately to reach that. All that any shading means is that you've got uphill and downhill; you've got a mountain and a valley. If you didn't have that you'd have a sheer cliff or a big flat mesa—a plane. I never use artificial light. The strongest and best light is light from the sky when it's cloudy, because there you've got something like a reflector, with the white clouds and the light pouring down. Leonardo knew that. If an artist really wants to model and see things correctly, he should go as far north as he can. It's a white light, and it's a beautiful light, because it shows the form of things. That is, if you're looking for the form. I'm not talking about abstraction. Nature is abstract. You don't create a nightmare or a dream. You don't have to. It's right here.

I got sidetracked. I might as well get back to the Pennsylvania Academy.

Why did you choose that school?

Because my dad went there. And at that time it was supposed to be almost a hundred percent fine arts. When I was there Charles Grafly was teaching, and Daniel Garber, Arthur Carles, and, oh, Henry McCarter, who was a classmate of my dad's. He taught composition. He was a classmate of Grafly's, but they hated each other. At that time Grafly was known as the best portrait man in sculpture in this country, and he was a realist. McCarter was talking about the abstract.

I put my canvas on the floor and painted a still life on it to make it flat. I wanted to have the things rise up. I thought: This vase is sitting on a table; it's not lying down flat on the table, it rises up. When it came time for McCarter to give me a criticism, I said, "This is supposed to be flat on the floor." He said, "You're not painting a rug." I said, "I know I'm not." He said, "You don't put it on the floor or the ceiling." And he shook his head. The next Friday when he came around, he said, "You're a real modernist. I've been thinking it over. That's all right." It wasn't a very good painting, but the idea was good.

What I'd really been looking for was what's back of painting as far as artists are like. I mean good ones, whether it's Bellini, Velázquez, El Greco, Michelangelo, Raphael (Raphael is a little sweet). You keep changing. Which you should do. I think you should admire a great number of artists at different periods, but I don't think you should copy them or be influenced by them. After all, they enjoyed what they were doing.

Why did you start viewing subjects from different angles?

Because I was fascinated. I thought: Why am I standing still? This apple or whatever it is has a viewpoint on the other side. Why do I confine myself to just one part of it? Why don't I explain it more? We had all this talk about Cézanne and other artists getting space, but I couldn't see where the hell the space was.

In "The Door" [*That Which I Should Have Done I Did Not Do*], I kept changing things aound. All you have to work with is light falling on an object. So on the molding I had the light falling on one thing. I thought: Why couldn't the light fall on the other side? Why do I always work the whole thing as if the light—heck. I'm just dealing with a fantasy, anyhow, or a vision. So I made certain sections with the light falling on the opposite side. And you get a reverse.

I made a brick wall for "The Window" [*Poor Room–There Is No Time, No End, No Today, No Yesterday, No Tomorrow, Only the Forever, and Forever and Forever without End*] and spent three days picking out the brick. Some of the bricks were burned where they had got too near fire, and there was a beautiful glaze like lava—yellow and green running down the sides. I picked out about five hundred or six hundred or maybe eight hundred bricks. For "The Window," I looked around for the sill or frame. I couldn't find anything I wanted, so I made one. I got old parts and put them together, trying to make up a portion a little bit narrower than usual, so it would have a little character outside of mine. For background, I got a not very good rug for the floor and an old bureau and I put a lamp on it and so forth.

How did you decide to use a window as the main . . . ?

I had painted "The Door" and had painted wood for ten years, and I didn't want to see any more wood as long as I lived. Before that I had painted a strong laborer. I called the painting "Room 203" [*And God Created Man in His Own Image*]. He posed for me for thirteen months. Well, after painting that guy for thirteen months, I didn't want to see any flesh. So I painted "The Door." So why did I paint brick? I wanted to get away from wood. And when I got through with brick, I didn't want to ever see a brick again.

Do you collect the objects in a painting with a particular reason in mind?

Well, yes—so they fit in. I use this old thing here, for instance. I don't want to have a new Tiffany pitcher, for God's sake (I don't like that new polished stuff anyhow).

Do you know what starts an idea for a painting?

Well, when I'm through with one and if I want to start another serious painting, if I need a model, the first thing I'd have to think about is if I can get a model and then, will the model stay with me. I don't want to get one that will die or become incapacitated or won't pose or is too fussy. If I want to make a figure piece, say, that would be the first thing to consider. Of course, if I want to make a still life, I'm on my own and they can't stop me. Then I try to run some subject through my head that might be of value to somebody philosophically, some conception other than painting. Something like a Childe Hassam—a fish and a bowl of grapes, for God's sake—to try to have something that will pertain to a phase of life that might have a little more meaning if possible. Then I go on from that.

And then you start to accumulate the objects that you use?

Once I know what I want. With "The Door" I kept collecting things. For instance, the doorstep was a tombstone. I got it in Naperville [Illinois] for thirty-five cents. My study of architecture came in handy here. I knew I'd have to have a threshold. I went down to the junkyard and finally found a nice brass thing that looked paintable, old, battered, not true. Then I thought a girl's hand would give it a little human interest. If you get a human being into a thing you have something closer. A piece of wood is not your roommate or your bedmate. I think it's better if you can tie it up somewhat with a person. So I got a girl with a small hand and posed the hand leaning. Symbolism. It could be a funeral wreath—anything. My mother had a very fine handkerchief of allover lace that probably belonged to her grandmother. It was very silly in size, unusable. It was white and I dyed it blue; I don't know why, except that I didn't want to paint a white handkerchief. I suppose I thought white would stand out too much, that it

Taylor & Dull, Inc.

Ivan Albright, *Portrait of Dorian Gray*, oil on canvas, 85″ x 40″, 1943–44. Collection of The Whitney Museum of American Art, New York.

would be too important. The brass key was from the door of my old studio, which I had built. I found an old door at a junkyard in Chicago. I didn't want to have an ordinary outside stock door three by seven feet made of white pine. I looked around until I found an old door that looked drab, like a Charles Addams or from a ghost house. One that would have a little character in itself, that had been painted and had started to fade. You want to pick something that looks as if it's lived its life. The funeral wreath. I got a cheap one so it wouldn't look like a gangster's funeral or a rich person's. I had to replace the calla lillies three or four times. The wires last only so long. You see, they're made for you to die and then be buried, not to have someone look at them for ten years. When I sent the painting to the Carnegie Institute I made a frame for it. It was terribly hard work. I wanted to line it with casket lining. I had to get a permit from the undertaker in Naperville to go to the casket company to buy it. At the company I bought that drab black cloth. When I asked how to put it onto a frame, the man said, "Well, what we use is library paste. They only want it for two or three weeks anyhow."

How did the long titles that you use come about?

My dad and all the artists of that early period—from 1903 up through 1912 to 14—used titles such as *Boy with Sunflower*, *Sunbonnet*, *Man Standing by River*. And I thought: My Lord, I would have loved to have been able to write. When I was a student at Northwestern University I tried to write. I got kicked out. I thought that there I not only had a chance to paint, but if I made the titles long enough I could write. In those days I was writing poetry. Do you want to hear a poem?

Sure. Do you still do it?

No, I haven't done it for many years. I have about three hundred poems.

When did you stop writing them?

More or less after I got married. I used to write a lot in Hollywood, under the piano, when I got drunk. There was Albert Lewin there. We were in Santa Monica on producers' row. Every

Saturday and Sunday they had these big cocktail parties. They never had writers there. They never had actors. You know, if they had had actors, they might try to get a job. For instance, once George Sanders went there and tried to get a job; he made an ass of himself. So it was mostly Jean Renoir, Anita Loos, people of that type. Al Lewin was a little guy, my size or smaller. And he could talk. He was professor of English at Harvard at one time. He had a good sense of amusement. He'd get up on a chair and tell story after story. Maybe there'd be about thirty people present. And Herb Staud was there. He was a musical chap; he had seventeen hits on Broadway. He'd get at the piano. Well, after, say, the nth drink I used to think: What the hell can *I* do? So I only had to take my paper and pencil and crawl under the piano and come up with a piece of poetry all in forty seconds or half a minute or a minute. Al Lewin would look at my poem and say, "Damn it! It's pretty good, anyhow." So, here's a poem I wrote, oh, many years ago:

A painter am I of all things
An artist who sees a door and chair
And sees them smooth things a flaw there
And sees them round things a hollow there
And colors are to him but the form within
He knows not but that the world is colored and strong
With light and shadow and forms that intertwine
And the sky is not blue to him as it runs over the meadows and trees
And the river is not held within its banks
As the colors swim over the land
And the tree is not a tree to him
But a song of beauty in the sky
And color is not just colors to him
But each a dream and a fantasy that makes unreal this world of yours to him
to this painter man.

Can you work on several paintings simultaneously?

This is the one I'm working on now. If you have two you would be running from one to the other; at least, I would. I tried that with "The Door." I had that and I had *Showcase Doll*, or something, started. I worked on one in the morning and one in the afternoon. I had these two setups. For *Showcase Doll*, I had a case made as if it were in a store, with the doll and lace and different stuff all around. And I found that I was running back and forth from one to the other. The light would get good over one—say, "The Door"—and I'd run over and work on it. Then I'd run back to the other one. Finally I said to myself, "For gosh sakes, Albright, make up your mind. It's got to be one or the other. Now which one?" Having no one else to decide for me, I chose "The Door." I worked on it for ten years.

The idea–the philosophy behind your pictures suggests an interest in philosophy in general. Are you interested?

No. The philosophy I use more or less goes with space and nature. Another man's philosophy wouldn't do me any good, but probably did the other man a lot of good. But if I can turn an object and make it go up and down, then I can create a feeling of motion, and with that feeling the object will take on a new dimension.

Do you feel that the objects in your paintings have symbolic meanings?

No. I know when I painted "The Door" I had it in Hollywood, and Sidney Janis came along and said, "You've got a whole lot of symbolism in it." "What do you mean?" I said, "I never tried to put any symbolism into anything." Maybe you're bound to get some, but I don't look for it, and I don't try to put any in. I think there's enough symbolism in making things move around, without my trying to put in a few clever little symbolisms. I don't think it's necessary.

You don't overpaint, do you?

No, never. Not on this stuff. To start a new painting, first I think of what I want to make. That may take a number of weeks. When I painted "Ida" [*Into the World There Came a Soul Called Ida*, 1929–30], I had her there for three weeks before I started to paint. I'd have her do everything: when I said "Pose," I didn't look at her; when I said "Rest," I'd look at her. I never hire professional models. I've never had one yet. The models I use are all amateurs, and they can't take these five-dollar-an-hour or fifteen-dollar-an-hour poses. They don't know them. They take natural poses. You can make them sleepy and tired, and they'll slump in a certain position that you know is more or less natural. If you wait until they get tired, the hands will drop down in a certain way. Then I study the light on them here and there. I don't make a sketch and try to have them fit the sketch. I work with the model and with light. Generally, in the studios I've had before this one, I've been able to pull every curtain up or down and control the light. Then when I find something I like, I mark the position on the floor with Scotch tape, the hour of day, how the clouds were, and about where the sun was. Then I monkey around, and if I find a better light I'll mark down the time, the clouds, and everything. Naturally, I know that it's just the law of averages if I get that lighting. Then I make a note of the clothes and so forth—so much open and so much closed and this and that. And I write down the poses. I don't try to make sketches. They don't amount to anything because I'm going to make a picture.

You mentioned off the tape that you wanted to continue talking about "The Window"?

In the first place, the setup covered an area of about fifteen by twenty feet in back of the window. Then I stood in front of the window. Now I have about fifteen major movements in the picture—swing this way and then foil against it; then minor things like the lamp, a flask, a bowl with flowers, like the chair with the three movements—and possibly forty to fifty minor movements controlled by the major movements.

What's a major movement?

A major movement would be swinging a big area in one direction, like a big arc; the whole window frame would swing one way. Then, to counteract it on the other side, I might have part of it swing one way and then swing back to have a force there. I make forces and then try to stabilize them so they won't be too violent. For instance, I have three beer bottles in one area. Each one, though fighting each other, is made from three different viewpoints, so they're contained. I'm trying to have it so you feel that you're walking in back of it and all through it, not just looking at it. I'm trying to put the observer in the picture, not outside of it. Though he *is* outside of it, I make him wander around through

Installation view of the exhibition *Works by Ivan L. Albright from the Collection*, 21 October–31 December 1978, The Art Institute of Chicago (*Courtesy of The Art Institute of Chicago*)

that room seeing the things from their different positions, as if he were in there. I'm composing with motion instead of with area, though naturally it becomes an area of flat paint.

What started you looking at things from different points of view?

It was gradual. The first pictures had a little of it. I had one, *Flesh* [1928]. It was just a glass bowl with water and the flowers upside down. It could go either way. We're taught about hollows. But who can tell which way it's hollow? It can be convex or concave. And later, with "The Door," I made the flowers from different heights, because I had to get them higher and from different angles. I found it had more volume and more space that way. Instead of trying to pretend there's space, I used the exact realism from a different direction, and I made one flower from one direction and the other from the other direction. I looked two ways in that picture.

Did that start by chance or by coincidence?

Well, no. As I told you, when I studied at the Chicago Art Institute, their color was mixed up with form, and color was mixed up with light. Hawthorne was always just color; he didn't understand when I said I wanted form. I was probably one of the first to go for form. From the form, I was trying to get more space than form. I was trying to get around the object. Trying to model it more than what you see. I'd walk from one position to another to try to reach around it to make it more sculpturesque, as it were. From the sculpturesque it turned into more motion. I'd walk further around, and I found that it gave more of an extending of the figure out toward you. I'm not trying to use distortion. I'm not distorting anything. If anything, I'm making the object more realistic by walking around it. An object has a million different viewpoints, and I'm taking a certain one. Now, say I'm going to paint a banana or a grapefruit or an orange or an apple on a table. That object doesn't have any size; it has all sizes. If you stand off fifteen feet, it's smaller. If you stand off far enough, it'll disappear. As it's disappearing, the color will become more and more neutral, until finally you'll have just a black spot. I'll walk about the same distance around it, so it will keep relatively the one shape. Say the object is three inches high; it'll keep that roughly. But I'll be painting the back of it and the front of it and trying to relate the two, but not too violently, because it won't work. But I *am* getting around the object. Well then, the object will have a tendency to try to get out of that shape. There's where the action happens when the observer looks at it. A lot of the objects I paint are trying to get back to their original shapes and that's where the force lies. And the job of the artist is to compose with these shapes and do what he wants with them. Naturally, that's where the artistic effort would be displayed.

Would you discuss your interest in the quality of light.

Ah, the quality of the light. Not working from sketches. I work moving a model around for, say, three weeks, or moving a still life around in a hundred positions. I use the skylight—top light. And then I like to concentrate. The more you make it smaller and smaller, the more you'll have a sharper light and more shadows, and it brings out more form. Here in Vermont, the light is fairly good. But it's better in Canada. I find that the farther north I go, the stronger and the whiter the light. I've painted in California a few times, and that is simply ghastly. It gets kind of an orange glow. It's impossible. I don't like it. I like a cold light, what some people might call a cruel light, the kind of light that no actress would want. I like a powerful white light on the head; this is the light that shows form the most. A steady light with white clouds reflecting down is, I think, the best light you can have.

In The Vermonter, *for instance, there is the luminosity of his hands and his face.*

I can't see that. But when I went to Chicago and looked at my pictures, I thought there was a little luminosity. I think that may be caused by getting close values. In painting a hand (and, incidentally, most artists paint terrible hands, including Rembrandt—horrible), you should make the fingers so they can move.

Do you look at the hands the same way you do an object?

Yes. It doesn't matter whether it's the head or the hand or a button or a piece of wood or the background or a brick or whatever. I try to make it have more feeling. In the painting "Room 203", I tried to put force in his eyes. I almost had to put it in myself, because people generally have a look of receding in their eyes, or they're hiding all their emotions back of them and trying to be secretive. You have to pull the emotions out of them.

In painting or anything, you cannot have hate. If you have hate, you destroy the picture and yourself. It doesn't work. You can have hunger, you can have thirst, you can have great feeling for texture, you can be sensitive to touch, you can be sensitive to color, but for the head you've got to be sensitive to love. Otherwise it will not work. I think that's the only thing. Now, that love won't change the shape, but it will add something. And you won't get that through feeling. You're going to have to just look and see the difference because it's extended out. Because, after all, when I'm painting you I'm not touching you; I'm off a ways. And this radiates out from a person. So it's in the air between myself and the object I'm looking at.

Don't you use a magnifying glass when you paint?

Well, I use it, yes. I paint under it. I'm a realist in that I want to paint that way. I'm an abstractionist in that I'm trying to have motion. But if I'm going to make a thing move, I'm not going to make a distortion. I don't want to move a distortion. I'm not interested in distortion. It's fun to play with, but it's just like a dream.

What would distortion be?

If I wanted to distort, I could make a coat this big or a sleeve. Like a Dali. I'm not trying to make a fantasy or a dream. I follow construction. I'm not trying to make a wonderful pattern like surrealism.

In a way, it's more real than real.

Yes. The reality is more than what a man can dream up. A man who makes a fantasy of surrealism thinks he can beat nature. And he can't. Because he's part of nature, and he's a small part. I'm just trying to follow nature and let nature come out. Which is a whole lot stronger, I think. I'm just the instrument of making it. In other words, I'm not an artist. No, it's true. I'm an observer. But I'm making people observe the way I want them to look.

But still, you don't use trompe l'oeil.

No. That would be like Hieronymus Bosch or something. That would be fun, too. But I would much rather do this and see how far I can go with it.

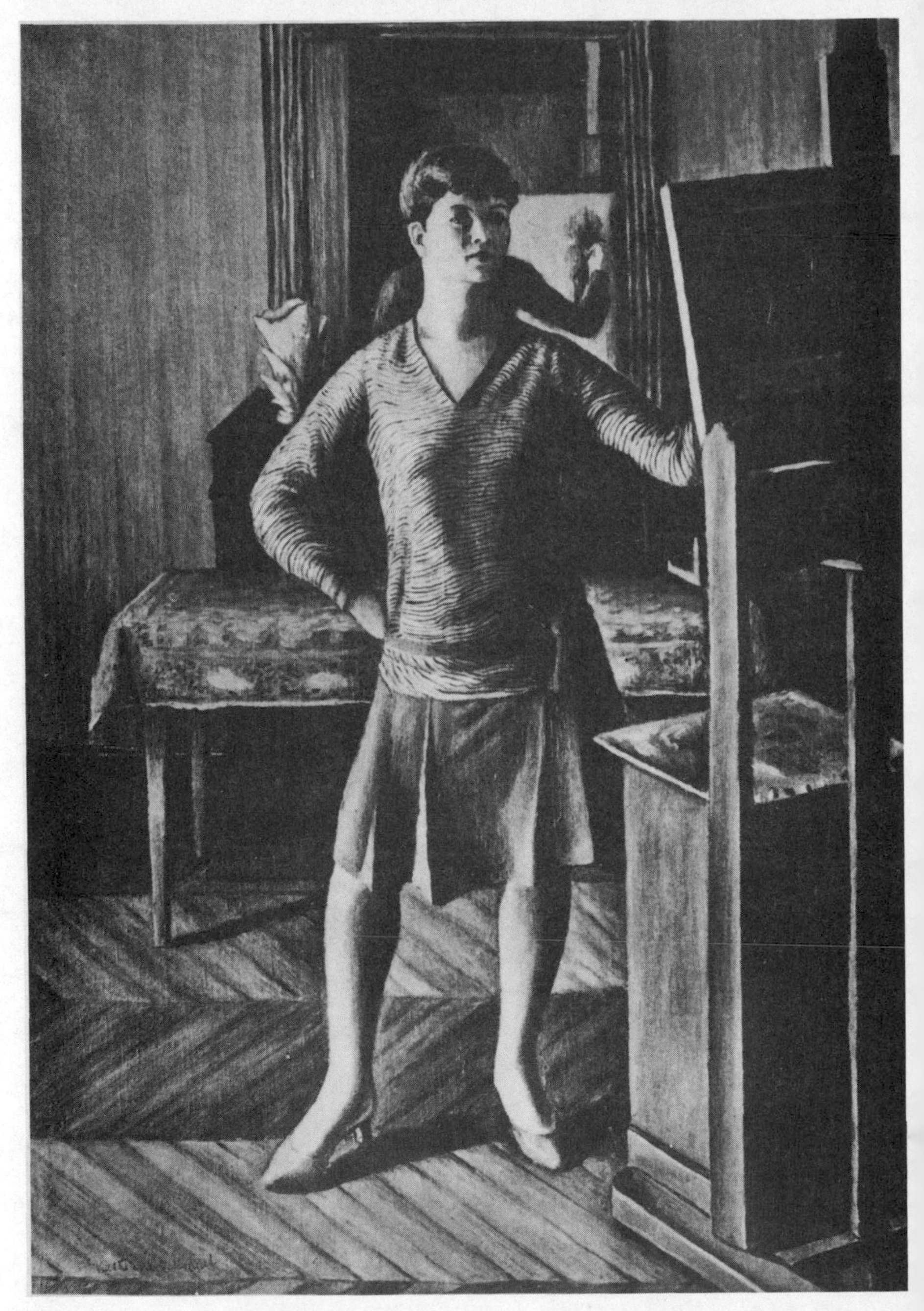

Katherine Schmidt, *Self-Portrait*, oil on canvas, c. 1929. Location unknown. (*Courtesy Zabriskie Gallery*, *New York*)

KATHERINE SCHMIDT

4

By retaining its conversational quality, a successful interview should capture the personality as well as the ideas of its subject. It should also conjure up in the reader's mind the ambience of the time in which the subject lived, the literary images of the day, the art favored, concepts of taste and style, the aspirations and evaluations of art and social history. In the following interview conducted on December 6 and 15, 1969, in her New York apartment, Katherine Schmidt (1898–1978) graphically describes the development of her interest in art as a child in Xenia, Ohio, where she was born, and her years as a young student at the Art Students League. She was married to Yasuo Kuniyoshi, whom she met at the league, from 1919 to 1932. In 1933 she married Irvine Shubert, a lawyer.

What was the life of a young woman at the league at the time of World War I? How were her aspirations influenced by those around her? In the words of Katherine Schmidt, a woman gifted with the ability to describe people and situations with warmth, insight, and charm, George Bellows, Kenneth Hayes Miller, John Sloan, and the young artists associated with them become vivid personalities. Schmidt discloses their cautious attitudes toward life and art. The world held simple promise for them. Lacking both informed cultural support and the ability and flair with which to express themselves, they were neither utopians nor visionaries. Unable to rise above the constrictions of social convention, their art suffers in today's critical evaluation, yet, possibly, it justly reflects their society. They were still of the generation torn by the difficulty of defining the boundaries of "commercial" art. They lacked the ability to infuse their art with the vitality they poured into their daily lives. The questions that beset the artists associated with the fauvist or cubist traditions were rejected. In their reliance upon history, not invention, social imagery and traditional painting techniques became crucial to their art.

Schmidt frequently refers to her own work, which manifests considerable development over the years. As a painter of the social realist school, she occasionally produced portraits, turning later to still life. Though she was persistent in her desire to be a painter of quality and exhibited regularly at the Downtown Gallery, the Whitney Museum of American Art, and elsewhere, she was never ambitious about establishing a public career. Her perceptive eye and refined discernment of her time aid us in realizing the images and atmosphere of those bygone days.

How did your family take to your going to the Art Students League?
Unkindly!

There weren't many galleries around at that time, were there?
There were the Montross and the Macbeth galleries—those are two that I remember, and Stieglitz and Daniel were the first to start with American things.

When did you start painting?
Heaven only knows. I remember the first paintbox I was given and a picture that my mother bought for me, one of those little prints, to copy. I worked very hard copying it. I made an awful mess all over the house, because I had never used oils before. Then they let me—I say "let me," because my father wanted me to take piano lessons, and I simply loathed the piano and didn't want to take lessons. I wanted to study art. Well, they finally allowed me to go to Saturday classes. For some reason or other I looked up the league. There were Saturday classes there. I went, I think, the last year in grammar school and my years in high school. And the only things you were allowed to draw were casts. Nothing else.

Saturday class was for the young. And it was there that I met my friend Ann Rector, who was very talented. I was not the least bit talented. I hadn't a glimmer of talent. But Ann was really gifted. She married Edmund Duffy, the cartoonist on *The Baltimore Sun*, and they were great friends of H. L. Mencken's. I used to visit Ann in Baltimore, where I met Mencken. He always kidded the pants off us—off me, at any rate. He referred to what we did as "handpainted oil painting."

What was the league like in those days?

In the Saturday class you drew casts. First you drew a man—a block figure—just to block out the general planes of the face with charcoal. Then the instructor would come in, rub it out, and say, "No. This is the way you do it." But she was a nice woman—Agnes Richmond—I was very fond of her.

Miss Richmond recommended F. Luis Mora. I went there in the afternoon. I can't remember anything except being thrilled with the whole thing. I had friends, of course. Molly Luce came in. She's a painter. At any rate, Luis Mora was a most gracious, pleasant, nice human being—very nice to everyone in his class. It wasn't the least bit like today. We used to be invited down to his studio on occasion. Everybody behaved themselves extremely well. And there was a lunchroom. There you got to know other people.

The classes were divided then into boys' classes and girls' classes. There weren't any mixed classes until later. I was in the women's life class taught by Mora.

Then the next year I'd really got my feet wet, and I decided—oh! I met George Bellows. Bellows was a wonderful person—a very warm person to young people; he loved them. And it didn't make any difference whether or not you were in his class. He used to have lunch with us in the lunchroom. If he liked you, you were invited to sit at his table. Though I wasn't in his class, I was always invited to have lunch at his table.

Did the teachers have lunch there?

No. Bellows also came from Ohio, and he would invite me when he invited his class. I'm sure I wasn't the only outsider who was invited, but I remember that I *was* invited. Well, I wanted very much to get into his class. I'd had enough of Mora, nice as he was. Bellows was much more exciting and more in tune with what was going on. He was beginning to be somebody. American art was just beginning to be something. You don't realize what a struggle it was. There were only the National Academy of Design, Eugene Speicher, Andrew Dasburg. A whole group of people was coming up. There was a ferment going on because people had been in France and had been influenced by the Impressionists and also by later developments. The independents were started here. John Sloan was a wonderful person—very friendly.

Well, I wanted to get into Bellows's class, but my father neglected to send the check for my tuition because it really didn't interest him very much. I don't think he did it out of malice. And when I went to the class, I was not in it. I think that was my first terrible sorrow—really grim disappointment. So I took the class next door. It was as near as I could get to Bellows's class.

Who was teaching your class?

Kenneth Hayes Miller. And I never loved Bellows after that. The next year I took George Bridgman's life drawing classes in the afternoon (I began to get ideas that I wanted to learn how to draw), and I went to Sloan's class at night.

How did Mora influence you? What did he do for you as a student?

I love nice people, and he was a lovely human being. He couldn't have been kinder to his students. But I never learned a single, solitary thing from him.

You didn't find him an exuberant teacher?

No. I found Miller very demanding and very exciting and also very interesting. At that time I think the Miller class combined. Then we began to develop friends who remained our friends. As I said, in the Miller class I had met Molly Luce, who later married Alan Burroughs. And I met Dorothy Varian. And there was Ann Rector, my friend from the league's Saturday class. Then I met Alexander Brook and Peggy Bacon, and they became *very* good friends of ours. I had met Yas Kuniyoshi by then. By the end of that year we had become very close; I was very interested in him.

How did you meet him?

In the class. And Peggy Bacon met Alex in the class. Everybody married everybody else, more or less. And then there was Lloyd Parsons, who was a very good friend of mine. And Arnold Blanch and Lucile Blanch. Lloyd Goodrich had been in the Miller class and would visit occasionally. I met him there, too.

To go back for a second–would you discuss Miller as a teacher?

Oh, yes. He was very good. A very strange, rather tight man, with a gimlety blue eye and a long nose. He seemed to smell your painting. And he was rather inclined toward intellectual pronouncements and aphorisms. But they always had some meaning. It was so strange—my love for Bellows and my wanting to be in *his* class, but after I started working with Miller I had absolutely no appetite at all to go into either Robert Henri's or Bellows's classes or any of that. Miller's was both emotionally and intellectually more demanding. You see, we didn't all work the same way. And we haven't. Kuniyoshi's work is not like mine. Alex Brook's work is not like Peggy Bacon's. All of us were enormously different. I think Miller's object was to bring out in you what was best for you to do, and to help you understand the precepts upon which painting is built, as he understood them.

So he really wasn't teaching what he knew. He was trying to make you discover your own talent.

He did both. He was a very original character. And even in the league days— I told you there was great ferment going on in the art world—there was a great division between those who were influenced by the French School and what I call good old American corn. Some of us went one way, some of us another. Kuniyoshi was much more intrigued by the French, because Jules Pascin was a friend of ours and his talent—everything about his talent was sensuous. Temperamentally, he had an affinity for French things. I remember we used to argue about who was the really key influence—Cézanne or Renoir? And we divided just in two. Some for Renoir, some for Cézanne. I have always felt that Renoir is a much greater painter. It's now becoming apparent, I think.

I remember our first trip to Europe in 1925. All our friends had been there in the early twenties. We were there for one year. We went with friends—Camby Chambers, Esther Andrews, and Sue Lawson, who was the wife of the playwright Howard Lawson. They were going over to meet Ernest Hemingway. They were very good friends of his. Yas and I were really shocked. We thought these people lived too high, drank too much wine, did too

Peggy Bacon, *The Ardent Bowlers*, drypoint on paper, 12 ⅜" x 21", 1932. Collection of The Whitney Museum of American Art, New York. *Top left*, Mr. and Mrs. Emil Ganso; *at the piano*, David Morrison; *with pipe*, Ernest Fiene; *leaning on the piano*, unknown; *bottom left*, Reginald Marsh; *on the stool*, unknown; *with glass*, Niles Spencer; *below Spencer*, Mrs. Wood Gaylor; *arms akimbo*, Katherine Schmidt; *below Schmidt*, Mrs. Niles Spencer; *upper center*, *bowling*, Bernard Karfiol;

much—and we couldn't afford it. We had a very hard time. My family disowned me when I married Yas. So we had a hard time earning a living. I had never done a thing. I didn't know what to do with a carrot when I was first presented with one. But I soon learned. We had to earn a living, and at that time it was very hard to do.

David Allison

seated on the couch, left, Alexander Brook; *next to Brook, with mug*, Edward Greenbaum; *behind them, with pipe*, Yasuo Kuniyoshi; *below*, Peggy Bacon; *at Bacon's right*, Dorothy Greenbaum; *right of upper center, picking up bowling ball*, Wood Gaylor; *right of Gaylor, with cigar*, unknown; *standing behind unknown, with mug*, Robert Laurent; *next to Laurent*, unknown; *below Laurent*, Mrs. Robert Laurent; *facing Mrs. Laurent*, unknown.

How long had you known Kuniyoshi before you married him?

About two years, two-and-a half years. We were married in Ogunquit, Maine. Yas had met Hamilton Easter Field—a very important influence in American art. He started *Arts* magazine and he was very influential in founding the Independents. He was the amateur *par excellence*. He was a musician. He wrote well. He painted. He really was the first to go after American primitive art in Maine. He was very generous to people he liked. He thought Yas was very talented, and he invited him to Ogunquit. He had a school; he had many buildings that he rented. And in exchange for Yas helping him, Field paid him a little bit of money, gave him a place to work, and gave him materials to work with. Yas did some of his first things there. It was Field who encouraged him. And that's how I happened to go to Ogunquit—because Yas had been there the year before. So my sister and I went there for the summer and rented a studio. Oh, it was something real then. There were artists. There were cartoonists. And everybody was serious. Now there's something so—the affluence of the country—the more neurotic and sick you are, the more you can paint.

How long did you study with Miller?

I became a friend of his. I was in the class perhaps for two or three years. But then, when I married Yas, we both had to work. Field at first had given us the studio in Ogunquit as a wedding present. But, and this was typical of him, in the middle of the winter he came to us and said (he stuttered), "K-k-k-Katherine and Yas-u-o, unfortunately I need that studio this summer. I have to rent it." That was a great shock to me because I believed that when people said something they meant it. Yas and I had a talk. He didn't agree with me. But I said, "I will not take another penny from this man. We are going to pay him rent. And I am going out and get a job. I've never had one, but I'll get one. And I think we both ought to do the same thing and be free. Who wants to be at the beck and call of somebody who is going to change his mind every fifteen minutes?" It just didn't suit my temperament. So I got a job running the lunchroom at the league. I wasn't very good at it. I kept it for two years, though. It paid only eighteen dollars a week; maybe I didn't even get that.

The teachers at that time seemed to be more involved in the lives of their students than they are now.

Oh, yes! They gave generously. We all helped each other. The first of this group to be really successful was Alexander Brook. Joseph Brummer took up Alex Brook, and Alex had his first show there. It was when Brummer first built the Fifty-seventh Street gallery. Alex would go out of his way to try to sell pictures for Yas, or do anything he could. And Bryson Burroughs was just extraordinary. He was so generous to his daughters' friends. Yas took to frame making, then to photography to make a living, and finally to teaching. But in those days practically everybody had to teach. And, except for a few, I think the same thing is true now.

You went to Europe in 1925?

Just after the first of the year. Yas had Japanese friends who got us a studio near the Porte de Versailles in a famous old building. Elmer Rice came to see us there, and years later he took someone out there and the building was still standing. It was right near the *abattoir*, where they killed horses for horse meat. We went up shaky wooden steps to the top of the building. It was absolutely crawling with bedbugs. Yas was very susceptible to bedbugs. They didn't bother me, but they made his life miserable. And though we paid for the studio, we decided that we simply couldn't stay there. We decided that I would use it as a work place. I've forgotten who said that someone on rue Premier was going away and we could have their studio. So we took it. We had planned to go to Italy in the fall and to the south of France in the winter, because Yas was doing lithographs. We got a great deal out of Europe. And we were very serious. We went to museums every morning and every afternoon. We looked at everything. When we traveled to look at pictures, we did nothing but look at pictures. Then we settled down. We came back to the south of France and got an apartment, also filled with bedbugs, but they burned candles or something—I don't know. There was an American artist there that I was fond of, but Yas didn't like him. He paints Maine—Marsden Hartley. He used to come in for tea practically every afternoon. And he would give Yas such a pain in the neck.

What was so difficult about him?

Well, he was a little bit—oh, I don't know—precious would be the word, I suppose. I liked him very much. I'll tell you a story about Marsden. Niles Spencer had got himself a brand new sports jacket. And it had long whiskers. It was just beautiful—so English and whiskery. And he met Hartley on University Place. Hartley looked at the jacket and felt the lapel, and he looked at Niles and said, "Pretty." Niles never got over it.

Did you get to know many French people–French artists–while you were there?

Never. Pascin was our friend. Occasionally he would have a party. But all the artists were Rumanians, Russians. Heaven knows, I don't think I ever met a French artist. Swedes, Japanese—there were a lot of Japanese there, by the way.

What was Pascin like?

Oh, again, he was another—you'll think I'm an awful bore. He was a most cultivated, sensitive, sophisticated European—a cosmopolitan. He could go anywhere. He had only one really dreaded fault. After a certain point he wanted to get himself into a terrible fight and get you into a terrible fight. We used to go up to Harlem quite often, and it was really dangerous because he would pick fights. We thought that he was looking for death. (Well, he killed himself, as you know.) He loved the general mélée. I remember one evening in Paris we started out at his studio. We went from place to place, and each time Pascin got a little bit worse. And then there'd be some commotion. People would begin coming up to the table. There was always something to worry about when you were with him in that kind of situation. He was an awfully good artist, by the way, according to my lights. I think that his work is going to remain with us. Very French.

John A. Ferrari

Katherine Schmidt, *Gift Wrapping*, oil on canvas, 18″ x 30″, 1960. (*Courtesy Zabriskie Gallery, New York*)

How much time did you spend in the south of France?

A whole winter. And I didn't like it. I had gone down there to paint landscape. I would walk for miles looking for something to paint. Everything was the wrong proportion. There wasn't a barn that looked right to me. Everything looked wrong. The olive trees were beautiful, but they weren't apple trees.

It wasn't American?

It wasn't America.

You were really attuned to American surroundings and ambience and objects.

Well, returning to Pascin, he started to argue with us about the fallacy of returning to this country—to the bourgeoisie and the barrenness of life here. And I made up my mind that after that trip I would never live abroad—ever. We went again to Europe in 1927 and 28. At that time Yas was very restless. And Pascin was after him all the time—told him that he would be making a great mistake to come back here. So I left. I said, "Yas, I will not stay here. It would just kill me. I'm an American. I don't care whether we're bourgeoisie or what we are. I belong there. I don't feel comfortable living abroad." So I came back. And Yas stayed through the fall and then decided he couldn't stay there either, and he came back.

What was it about Europe that you found so unsettling?

As I said, I would go out and walk for miles and never find anything to paint. The idiom was wrong. It didn't look natural. It wasn't right. You know, olive trees are the most beautiful things if you're just sitting on a terrace with a glass of sherry or something in your hand and looking at them (though you don't drink sherry in France, you drink vermouth), seeing the silvery light. Most beautiful. But it isn't anything that I want to paint. I like to take something that isn't beautiful, like my leaves. They look like old dried-up things until—I can see something in them that's rewarding. There's been a cleavage, I think, between the French influence and American corn. And I certainly belong to American corn.

What's your definition of American corn?

Well, we're not very well trained. Do you know Thomas Nast? I think he's just as great as Daumier, but he isn't *known* to be so. But will be in time. I've got a great many of them. I'm a great admirer of Nast. Reg Marsh and I used to haunt Fourth Avenue to pick up his old prints. That is what I call American corn. He trained himself. And, you see, there is that strain. Kenneth was that, too, though he wouldn't admit that he was corny. But I admit it.

What about Marsh?

Marsh was the son of a painter, an accomplished mural painter. Now, artists who are the children of artists are already sophisticated. Take the artist who is so successful, and deservedly so—Andrew Wyeth—who paints the rather dry Pennsylvania things. He is a beautiful painter. He is the son of a painter. And *his* son is a painter. They start with a sophistication. I'm a little girl from Ohio; I don't start with any sophistication. I start exactly the opposite.

But what about the people at the league?
Yes, but nobody trained me.

What about Bridgman?
Oh, I liked him very much.

As a teacher?
You had to do things by formula with him. And I resented that and always rather balked at this formula idea. He stopped me in the hall one day and said, "Miss, I really don't want you to think of me as an old fogey. I know better, but this is the easiest way to make you learn." He was an intelligent man. He knew how to teach people. His best pupil I think was Edmund Duffy, the cartoonist on the *Baltimore Sun*. It was just that Bridgman didn't want me to think that he was such an old fogey, but that this was one way of teaching. And I suppose at the league we belonged to what would be known as the swinging group. I mean we were the first of the younger group to have shows and so on. There was quite a group in that period just before the twenties.

Did you get to know Sloan?
I loved Sloan. I think that the people he did the most for were the people who had learned to paint in the academy fashion with La Grippe and Drew, and Sloan would tear into their work and just put them on their feet. Nothing superficial. No tricks of turning over your brush for paint or any of that kind of nonsense. You had to be sincere. And the people he loved most were the butchers and bakers and candlestick makers who came to the evening classes after working hard all day. He would work so hard over them. They were very naive. He loved their sincerity.

Who was the most important to you as a teacher at the league?
Miller.

Do you think that knowing him personally had an effect on you?
Oh, yes. Yas was Kenneth's pupil, too, you see. But then, as with fathers and sons, once a certain point is reached they break and want to have nothing to do with one another. Yas got so that he just didn't want to have anything to do with him. That was

very difficult for me. I used to go to Miller's tea parties that he had every Wednesday afternoon, and, by George, you were *supposed* to turn up. They were in his studio. This was after he moved from Twenty-third Street. He had a studio on Fourteenth. And everybody would be there from Theodore Dreiser to Sterritt to friends, relatives from Kenwood, students, and a lot of lady artists.

Was it a salon?

Well, no. If you had known Kenneth and had seen the Morris chair, the rubber plant, the mission table—it had a style all its own. It had nothing to do with a salon.

But the continuity—every Wednesday afternoon.

Yes. But, again, that doesn't fit in with American corn. No American has a salon.

Where did you get the idea of American corn?

Oh, I always think up crazy ideas.

What painters interested you besides the early Italians?

My great enthusiasm was Titian, Rubens, Bellini. Bellini especially—well, he's a little later. I always loved Bellini. And Mantegna. But I pay very little attention to that now. I usually keep a Rubens sketch in the studio so I can have something to remind me of what I like to look at.

When you were a student, what painters interested you particularly?

Renoir I loved. I still love Renoir. He's a beautiful painter and a beautiful artist. Cézanne was never a beautiful painter. He painted adequately. I think the great Renoirs have much greater design than anything Cézanne ever thought of. I remember [in the Museum of Fine Arts] in Boston they had a Rogier van der Weyden, a Renoir—*Dance at Bougival* [1883]—a Velázquez, and something else, hanging in four corners. The Renoir stood up with all of them.

How did you become involved with the Whitney Studio Club in 1923?

How it came about I really don't know. So many of us just

gravitated in that direction. There was probably no place else to go.

How did you meet Juliana Force?

At the club. And I worked for her for quite a while. I ran the sketch class for the club for a couple of years. Edward Hopper was my pal in the sketch class. He never missed.

What was he like in those days?

Sour as always. I was very fond of him, but he was very laconic and had not much to give. But he always turned up for sketch class.

I haven't said a word about the cartoonists in Ogunquit. And Walt Kuhn and the Dicky Bird Club. I'd forgotten about it—haven't thought about it for years. This summer I had a birthday and my husband [Irvine Shubert] asked me what I'd like. I said, "I don't know. I don't think I want anything." And he said, "I'll give you a check and whenever you see something you want, you get it." Well, we had made a study for him, and we had to get a new lamp. We went over to New Bedford. There's a wonderful antique dealer there, and we had bought a very nice old lamp from him. But the top row of crystals was wrong and he promised to get me some new ones. I went over to get them, and when I got there I saw two green lusters. And I said, "Those are going to be my birthday present. But the only trouble with it is that it certainly is 'dicky bird.'" "Dicky bird?" Irvine said. "What in the heck is dicky bird?" And I explained that Walt Kuhn (and all the rest of us) used to call everything that wasn't art—ornaments, that sort of thing—we'd call them "dicky bird." It wasn't art. It's decoration—ornamentation of some sort. Now Walt was a "corny" character and a very shrewd, very able man. We saw a great deal of him in Ogunquit. He had a house there. But that's what dicky bird is.

And after we all got married, the boys and girls used to divide up—Kuhn, Louis Bouché, Emil Ganso, Yas, and, I guess, Niles, too—they had a club they called the Dicky Bird Club. Pascin would go to it. And they would make drawings. Sometimes they would make naughty drawings. Spend the whole evening doing nothing but that. Or they might get a model and draw. They had a whale of a good time. Just the boys.

What was it like in 1929, during the crash?

That year we built a house in Woodstock—1928 or 1929. We had saved our money, and I had inherited a little. We put it into building a house on Ohio Mountain. Yas loved Woodstock. He had a lot of friends there. I did, too. Everyone welcomed us. The older artists—Eugene Speicher, Henry McFee—they made a big fuss over Yas. At any rate, to answer your question: 1929 and the 1930s, while they were awful years because the people around us suffered a great deal, didn't seem very different to me because I had the same job at the Whitney. I ran the sketch class, as I said, and did odd jobs for Mrs. Force.

How would you describe the Whitney Studio Club?

Oh, it was so gay! I remember our younger years as always being spring. Everybody met to dance and have fun. Everyone was so alive. You did not have to be so careful of your opinions. You could say, "I don't like this," very flatly, and expect the other person to say, "I do," and have it out. But without any ill feeling. Now it's a matter of, "You're my enemy." There was a much more childlike, innocent quality of fervently held beliefs. I told you about the terrible arguments that went on about who was the greater artist, Cézanne or Renoir. We'd practically pull each other's hair out over that.

Most of the people who went to Woodstock were not involved with abstract painting, were they?

No. When we were there around 1927, 1928, 1929, the most successful people were Speicher and McFee. Dasburg had been there before them. And there was very little abstract art. The dominant influence I think was a trickle of Cézanne and a trickle of Renoir. But the other aspects of French painting didn't make any dent.

That group was very interested in the old masters, wasn't it?

Well, Henri, who was a friend of theirs, was very interested in

Velázquez, but not interested in the old masters. The teacher who was interested in the old masters per se was Kenneth Miller. I don't think Henri was remotely interested in the Italians or Rubens. And Sloan was much more interested in the naive, sincere effort of a person to create something. He didn't give a hoot about tradition, as far as I could see.

Which was the most influential museum in American painting through the 1930s–the Whitney or the Modern?

I think the Whitney was more important in the beginning in maintaining, buying, supporting people. But the Modern, as far as influence goes, was by *far* the greater influence and more meaningful as an expression of the time. Alfred Barr was very sensitive in knowing in which direction the trend was going. I think in its time it will run itself out. Most of the things the Modern encouraged will not be found to be as valuable as it thought. I *do* think that it has had meaning as far as architecture and interior design—the decorative arts. It's had a great influence. And with the nouveau riche it has been very important, because how else can they spend all their money?

Walker Evans, photograph by Jerry L. Thompson, 1974.(*Courtesy Jerry L. Thompson*)

WALKER EVANS

5

Walker Evans's ambition was to be a writer. Born in St. Louis, Evans (1903–1975) was raised and schooled in Kenilworth, a Chicago suburb. At Williams College, his association with students of literary taste, who read the modern writers they had discovered outside their classrooms in little magazines, sustained and increased his aspirations. "I was," he said, "almost a pathological bibliophile." In 1926, Evans went to Paris, enrolled in the Collège de France, and audited classes at the Sorbonne. He was "intensely a Frenchman...determined not to speak English...dressed like a Frenchman even." For reasons similar to those given by Katherine Schmidt (*q.v.*), he rejected the life exemplified by F. Scott Fitzgerald and Gerald Murphy, saying, "I was in flight from that...I wouldn't have gone near it." In 1927, when he returned to the United States to live in New York, Evans sought part-time jobs at night so he could be free to photograph during the day.

On the brink of the Depression, in 1928, Evans made his first serious photographs. He soon evolved a style, directly confronting the subject, that was crisply focused, luminous, geometric, of pyramidal design, and generally unpeopled. Empty interiors hint of their occupants' pasts: "I do like to suggest people sometimes by their absence.... I like to make you feel that an interior is *almost* inhabited by somebody." He would, however, photograph people selectively, frequently furtively. His images pile up on the page in a close shallow space. Such stacking negates the natural vistas of city and landscape.

The Depression, Evans said, "was rather good for some kinds of artists, me included. It took away the temptation to be commercial and go into business. It gave you leisure. There's a detachment that an artist must have. Adulation is a handmaiden of fame and fame is very bad." He felt that "few sophisticated people were attracted to photography because it... had a bad name for itself." At one time, Evans had a "flirtation with advertising photography at N. W. Ayer. It made me sick. After all, my father was in the advertising business. I knew what it was like. I didn't want to be like that."

Evans's photographs, patterned in tones of gray to black and white, trigger the imagination and establish at the same time the photographer's personal vision of America, one that was to influence many younger photographers. Finally, his images were made, not with the pen, but with the quick shutter in the camera's eye.

In this interview, which was conducted on October 13, and December 23, 1971, both at his home in Connecticut and at his apartment in New York, Evans summarized his attitude toward life: "In a way, everything interests me, and nothing."

Did you pursue your interest in wanting to become a writer at Williams College?

Yes. I became intensely literary in that one year. But it had almost nothing to do with the English classes in school. It was outside. Just look who was publishing then! That's who I was reading: D. H. Lawrence, Virginia Woolf—all those people. I was in the class of 1926. This was taking place in 1922 and 23. T. S. Eliot was just coming up. You can be sure that Williams didn't teach you those. You had to go and get them. We did.

You knew what was modern.

You're damn right. I was right there. I now pride myself on that.

Was it through your friends, or was it your own discovery?

Both. It always is. These things generate. I'm fatalistic about it. I think the boys that *should* know T. S. Eliot as he's coming up *do* know him.

How did you happen to go to Paris?

I'll bet you George Moore sent me to Paris. Of course, it was. There, again, I just sensed that that was the place. And I was right.

What happened in Paris?

I was very poor and obscure and quite unhappy and lonely. It wasn't what most people think of as Paris in the golden age. Not for me. But I was intensely excited about and interested in the ferment. I felt there was a very exciting artistic period in Paris in the twenties. It was in the air. I lived on the Left Bank. I lived with a student and knew what was going on.

Did you know any writers or painters?

No. You see, I felt very much outside of all that because I was nobody. And I wasn't doing anything. I was absorbing it all. The thing that kept me from knowing the Americans was that I was anti-American. I was not fleeing them, but I disdained the moneyed, leisured, frivolous, superficial American, like Scott Fitzgerald. I wouldn't have paid any attenton to him at all, however famous and successful a writer he was, because he wouldn't speak French and had materialistic values. He was in love with the rich. I thought this was terrible. Also, they were older. Ernest Hemingway was five years older. That's a lot at that age.

I did go to Sylvia Beach's bookshop [Shakespeare and Company]. I used to see James Joyce. I used to talk to Sylvia. She sensed that I knew my Joyce, and she said she'd introduce me to him. But I was scared to death to meet him. I wouldn't do it. He came in, and I left the shop. He was my god. That, too, prevented me from writing. I wanted to write like that or not at all. I think he ruined many a young man. He was our god to the last man. We would die for him. Oh, yes, we took that damn seriously. That was literature.

You came back in 1927. What happened on your return?

I had odd jobs. I guess soon after that I got hold of a camera and got passionately interested in that. I do remember having jobs at night at two different places, one on Wall Street and one at the New York Public Library, so I could have days free. I photographed during the day.

How did the camera appear?

I really don't know. As a boy I had a cheap little camera, and I had gone through the hobby-photography experience, developing film in the bathroom and so on. I think it came from painters. Several of my friends were painters. And I had a visual education that I had just given myself.

Who were the painters?

Well, nobody that you'd speak of now. I was always interested in artists. I was just drawn to them. Added to that is the fact that I think I associated it wth forbidden fruit. It was not the thing to do. So I would do it.

The bohemian life and adventure.

Yes. Exactly. I was the young bohemian artist, absolutely typical. Though at the time I didn't know it. But I was.

What did you photograph?

I think I was photographing against the style of the time, against salon photography, against beauty photography, against art photography. Even including Alfred Stieglitz. I was doing nonartistic and noncommercial work. I felt, and it's true, that I was on the right track. I sensed that I was turning new ground.

Did you know the photographers of that time?

No. I wasn't drawn to the world of photography. In fact I was against it. I was a maverick. As a matter of fact, I really think I was on the right track right away, and I don't think I've made very many false moves. I now feel almost mystical about it. I think something was guiding me, was working through me. I feel that I was doing better than I knew how, that it was almost fate. I really was inventing something, but I didn't know it.

You hadn't studied photography?

No. I worked at it. I taught myself photography. I got all the books and also talked to anybody that knew anything about it. And I was interested in the technique.

What were the qualities of salon photography that aggravated you or that you reacted against?

Conventionality, cliché, unoriginality.

What about Stieglitz and Camera Work*?*

Stefan Hirsch, a painter, was living in Brooklyn Heights. I got to know him. He knew Stieglitz and knew that I was photographing and evidently liked my work. He sent me to Stieglitz with a note saying—I still remember this—"Please look at this young man's work." That was my first encounter with Stieglitz.

It was disastrous on both sides. We didn't like each other. I fell in love with Georgia O'Keeffe. Well, you can say that in quotes. Actually, I did without knowing it. I was very taken with her because she was nice to me and was sensitive and beautiful. I was probably starved for that kind of thing. Here was this beautiful woman—Stieglitz wasn't there when I arrived. She began talking to me with kindness and understanding and, naturally, I was crazy about her. I opened up and spent half an hour talking to her before Stieglitz came in. I showed her my work.

Did he like what you were doing?

He was bored and tired. And furthermore I wasn't sycophantic or worshiping of him. He saw that immediately. And by that time he was pretty spoiled and wanted that and needed it and used it. So he had no time for me at all. He said, "Very good. Go on working. Goodbye."

It didn't take.

No. And I was very shy. I only went because I felt I owed Hirsch the presentation of his letter. And having done it and having found that there wasn't anything going on between Stieglitz and me, I never bothered to go back, in spite of the fact that I was loving Georgia from afar. She was marvelous. She was really charming. Though I wasn't interested in her painting very much. She was just a hell of a warm, nice woman, really generous and really giving, really sensitive.

Were you taking photographs during this time?

I had a passion for photography. I could think about nothing else—reading and photographing.

Were there older photographers that interested you?

No. Nothing. Well, I did get excited over one Paul Strand picture. I remember his famous *Blind Woman* excited me very much. I felt that that was the thing to do. That really charged me.

Do you remember what appealed to you in that photograph?

Sure. It was strong and real, it seemed to me. And a little bit shocking—brutal.

Were those qualities that you worked for?

Well, that's what attracted me in art. I would read a book like Knut Hamsum's *Hunger*, and that was a joy because I thought it was real. It really wasn't, but my lack of judgment led me to believe that, since I had had a genteel upbringing, real life was starvation, and that writing about it was *honest*. That's all wrong, but that's what I thought. I thought to photograph the *Blind Woman* was the thing to do.

It was very close to that time that you got involved with Lincoln Kirstein, Ben Shahn, and Muriel Draper.

It was Lincoln who introduced me to the great Draper woman. There's a very perverse side to Lincoln, you know; he loves all sorts of funny business. That certainly was high cheese.

She was a remarkable woman and very useful in the education of young men like me at that time. I must say it. Though she was putting on an act, and it was completely artificial and phony to the fingertips, there was still something good in it. She was the great mother of all artists. Anybody who was an artist could come to her house. And that's a good thing, too. There ought to be a house like that now. It was an imitation French salon, indiscriminate, but the nearest thing we had. And that's necessary in a culture. A lot went on. A lot of it questionable. It was anything but a respectful house.

What about Lincoln Kirstein?

I'll be damned if I remember how I met him. But probably at—I was going to say at the Drapers', but I think he must have taken me to Muriel's house. There was a sort of false start in our relationship. I had a night job in a bookstore, and he used to come in there. I'd love to know, myself, where I met Lincoln Kirstein. Oh! He had the *Hound and Horn*, and I may have gone to try to sell him pictures. He published photographs, and I may have seen them. And he did publish pictures of mine. Or he may have come to me. He was interested in photographers and in unknown artists, and he may have found out that I was an unknown artist and looked me up.

What about Ben Shahn?

People get drawn together when they're meant to. Shahn and I met at somebody's house on Columbia Heights in Brooklyn. I know that. There was a doctor there who picked me up on the street because he was a photographer. He had an assumed name. He called himself Yago Galston. He was a doctor who wouldn't practice.

Didn't you share a studio with Shahn for a while?

I did, indeed. Not only did I share a studio—he had an apartment with a basement, and I lived in the basement. And later, across the street, we all had a studio with Lou Block, the three of us, but mostly Ben and me. I had the back, and he had the front—23 Bethune Street. I remember it so well.

What was it like, sharing space with Shahn?

Well, we had a great attachment to each other, Shahn and I. But he was an overpowering man, which I began to resent. He was too strong for me. But I knew I was getting educated. After all, the little boy from Kenilworth, Illinois, had never seen anybody like that, the son of a Russian immigrant right out of the streets, and

Walker Evans, *Greek Revival Doorway*, *N.Y.C.*, photograph, 1934. (*Courtesy Sidney Janis Gallery*, *New York*)

tough. All the things I thought were exotic and fascinating. It was marvelous. I was very attracted to his work. I loved it. I still do to this day. He was a very clever, interesting artist. We both had the same kind of an eye, really. That's why he got interested in photography. He used to shamelessly make pictures from photographs. Newspapers or his own. That's why he took it up.

What about Hart Crane? How did you do the photographs for The Bridge [*1930*]*?*

I think he must have picked me up in the street, too, in Brooklyn Heights. That's where he was living. Anyway, we did get to know each other. He was in love with the Brooklyn Bridge, and he loved those photographs.

How did the Depression affect you?

I have a theory, in retrospect, that it was good for us all. It gave us time without the pressure of getting a job. It allowed a crowd of people who were on the road to being artists to stay artists instead of going off into Wall Street or Time, Inc. I stayed on; I probably would have anyway, because I was very willful about it. I was going to be an artist, and I was goddamned if I was going to be a commercial businessman or a success at anything else.

What about the Federal Art Project?

I was on the Resettlement Administration, which became the Farm Security Administration.

Was it a rewarding activity?

Oh, gosh, yes! Why not? Of course, it was. A subsidized freedom to do my stuff! Good heavens, what more could anyone ask for? And the result shows it. That whole hot year I was tremendously productive. I developed my eye, my feelings, about this country. Oh, yes, that was great for me!

Do you think that that period influenced subsequent work?

Yes, in the sense that inevitably I was growing and getting experience. Sure, I developed. But, mind you, this development wasn't in the eyes and minds of the federal government at all. It was all an accident that as an artist I found this development there. They had that thing set up for an entirely different reason.

Didn't Kirstein commission you to make some photographs of architecture?

That seems to be part of the legend. I wouldn't put it that way. He took me off on a trip. He and particularly Jack Wheelwright—John Brooks Wheelwright—were interested in a romantic revival and other unstudied, undiscovered styles in American architecture. I was a photographer, and Kirstein had the natural idea to go and photograph these things. I didn't think twice about it. I was perfectly free and had a camera, and if he wanted to finance the trip that was all right with me. We went in his car to various places, not too far. I think he was still an undergraduate.

It's something I wouldn't have done myself. It was interesting chiefly because of Kirstein, and it was a perfectly respectable thing to do, that is, documenting architecture. And it taught me a lot. In fact, it introduced me to a knowledge of how to appreciate and love and respond to various kinds of architecture and architectural styles. I had had a natural attraction to architecture, but no experience. This gave me a certain sophistication. I was always interested in architecture and in the way buildings looked. But that was as far as it went. I think that came from my father, who was a frustrated architect.

What about the photographs you were taking during the thirties?

I was working by instinct, but with a sense, not too clear, but a firm sense that I was on the right track, that I was doing something valuable and pioneering aesthetically and artistically. I just knew it. And Kirstein helped me a lot. He used to tell me what I was doing. He was a very perceptive critic and aesthete.

Were you interested in any specific kinds of equipment?

I've always been interested in cameras. I'm even interested, a little bit too much, in the technique of photography. It's a fascinating thing, but it hasn't much to do with art, and an artist had better stay away from it, not get absorbed in it. It's too absorbing. You can do all kinds of tricks. It's just better not to. I am after mastery of what I want to do. And I insist on that in teaching. I think you've got to know what you're doing and be on top of it and do it well. There's no excuse not to know the technique well. But I don't teach the technique. I say you should go out and do it somehow or other, get it yourself.

How would you define art in photography? What is the quality that's being defined?

You define it in photography the same way you do in painting or literature. Nobody does it convincingly, that is, exclusively. You know perfectly well that, in writing on aesthetics and in art criticism, there are some very profound and satisfactory treatises that are the essence of criticism. Photography is very weak in that. There isn't any in photography to speak of.

What are the qualities that differentiate fine-art photographers from commercial photographers?

I'll preface my answer by a remark that has come to me lately. I've been thinking about it. In my time, in the thirties or when I was moving into this, it so happened that very few men of taste, education, or even general sophistication ever touched photography. Nobody ever says that very much. But that has a lot to do with the history of photography. And the fact that quite a few people of real discrimination, taste, and generally superior critical minds have come into it. We don't often talk about how damn few superior minds were ever in it. Also, it was a disdained medium. It was laughed at and misused and corrupted by everybody. My poor father, for example, who had a conventional attitude toward all the arts and all that, decided that all I wanted to do was to be naughty and get hold of girls through photography, that kind of thing. He had no idea that I was serious about it. And respectable, educated people didn't. That was a world you wouldn't go into. Of course, that made it all the more interesting for me, the fact that it was perverse.

You had a show at the Museum of Modern Art in 1933?

The one in 1938 was more important. That's the one I remember, because to my mind it was the first big photography show that I'd had, and it was the first big one that the museum gave. I don't consider that business about architecture in 1933 a show.

Did it affect your photographic career?

Oh, very much. It was like a calling card. It made it. The catalogue, particularly, was a passport for me. It established my style and everything. Oh, yes. And as time went on it became more and more important. It turned out to be a landmark. It was particularly important because, as I say, more than I realized, it established the documentary style as art in photography. For the first time it was influential. The Modern is a very influential place.

You refer to the "documentary style." How do you define it?

It's a very important matter. I use the word "style" particularly, because in talking about it many people say "documentary photo-

Installation view of the exhibition *Walker Evans: 250 Vintage Prints*, 6 January–4 February 1978, Sidney Janis Gallery. (*Courtesy Sidney Janis Gallery, New York*)

graph." Well, literally, a documentary photograph is a police report of a dead body or an automobile accident or something like that. But the style of detachment and record is another matter. That, applied to the world around us, is what I do with the camera, what I want to see done with the camera.

But there's a certain attitude or feeling that one gets from looking at your photographs, because of the way that the camera looks straight out. There are no tricky angles. It's a very straightforward approach. It's just a certain moment in time. Did you develop that consciously?

That's a very important matter, too. That took time to establish. I was doing it instinctively, because I thought that was the way I ought to be doing it, without thinking very much. And I also was very lonely in it, because nobody thought of that or recognized it very much. Now it's been vindicated more than in most cases. I happen to be an artist who has been treated justly by time and by the world. My own style has been established and credited to me. Lots of inventors, which a stylist is, don't get credit for their inventions. In this case, I did, luckily.

There is a special quality of light in your prints.

I'm interested in the style of light. Of course, light almost is photography, so I care about what it is. And there are all kinds of light. There's high noon and sunlight and cross light. I like to work in direct but subdued cross light. Dawn and dusk are the times to work with a camera, I think. But not romantically.

Shadows are always quite apparent.

I think that's important. You can't always do that in architecture, because you have no control over where the sun is and where the building is placed. But I've noticed, almost unconsciously, that, if I can, I get the light falling in a certain way on a facade.

Are you interested in letters and in words?

More and more that's coming to a head right now. Oh, yes, lettering and signs are very important to me. There are infinite possibilities, decorative in themselves, such as popular art, folk art, and as symbolism and meaning and surprise and double meaning. It's a very rich field.

Do you know why they are important to you?

No, I don't. I think, in truth, I'd like to be a letterer. And then, broadly speaking, I'm literary. The sign matters are just a visual symbol of writing.

Do all your prints come from the same negative size?

I have evolved more or less into a Rolleiflex man. That's two-and-a-quarter format.

Do you prefer that over a thirty-five?

Yes. If you handle it right you can make a two-and-a-quarter negative look almost like an eight-by-ten contact. You can't quite do that, or *I* can't do it, with a thirty-five millimeter. It's an entirely different kind of photography.

Do you print the full negative?

Not always. I crop if I feel like it. In fact, I don't like square pictures. I very often find they're oblong. I don't believe in manipulation of any photograph or negative. To me it should be strictly straight photography and look like it, not be painterly, ever.

Straightforward printing.

Yes. Photographs should be photographic.

You're not interested in photographing people in the way you are buildings, are you?

I'm not interested in people in the portrait sense, in the individual sense. I'm interested in people as part of the pictures and as themselves, but anonymous. I really disapprove of photographing celebrities or known beauties. I do it every once in a while, but I think it's—I can't quite put my finger on it, but I don't feel right doing it. I don't think a photographic portrait is true. The worst of it is something like Karsh. But even a portrait man is doing something that is false to begin with. And the business of photographing celebrities is too easy.

But don't you think it's possible to document people in a photograph that...

It's almost never done. Yes, I do. I think it should be donc, but never done that way. And those things are valuable. But I say that anybody can do it. I wish I had done more, now. There are many people that are no longer around that I would like to have photographed. But I do have a psychological block about it. I haven't analyzed it very much. I was around Hemingway a little bit, but I would never bring out a camera and photograph him, out of regard for him really, as too obvious a thing to do. I thought too much of our relationship to throw a camera into it.

That would make some change then, wouldn't it?

Well, it's probably pride, too, and ego. My own private ambition comes in there. I don't want to do the easy thing. I want to do much more difficult things.

How did you decide to do the subway riders series?

That has a great deal to do with portraiture. That's my idea of what a portrait ought to be, anonymous and documentary. A straightforward picture of mankind, not of a celebrity, not journalism.

So it's really unposed?

You see, that raises journalism. The moment you do somebody at an editor's request or because that person is famous, you're doing journalism.

In the subway series, you don't get the feeling that they were aware of being photographed.

They weren't. I arranged that by going at a certain season of the year when you can wear a topcoat and sort of half hide the camera under it, going at a time of day when the subway isn't too crowded, figuring out the lighting and all that. Nobody asked me to do it. It's value to me—it was a project for love.

Are a lot of your photographs done for that reason?

Yes. I'm very noncommercial, rather fiercely so. I'm mad at commercial people. I get into terrible fights. Even recently, *Life*, in its insidious way, sent people up to give seminars at Yale. I was up in arms about it, because I knew it was a very corrupt thing to do. They would do some talent hunting on the side. That made me furious. They were using Yale.

What have you been doing at Yale, and what are your feelings about teaching photography?

I went to Yale skeptically. Jack Tworkov called up and asked, "Do you want to be a visiting critic?" I said, "I don't know what it is. I'll investigate it. What is it?" I got up there and found that I wasn't expected to do much except look at some work and criticize it. Then I discovered that it was more than that, more rewarding, too. The project with the students was unexpectedly a very rich thing for me to go into. Rich for me. For a self-made teacher, I'm not much of a teacher, but I've had some effect on the boys, and it's been great for me.

I assume that anybody who gets to me is on top of technique, has mastered it. If something is bad, I'll say so, I'll criticize it, rather severely in fact. They complain. But otherwise they don't pay much attention to it.

You talk about their eye and their vision and...?

Yes. It's the seeing that I'm talking about.

What might you tell a student?

On the lowest level, I would tell him he's on the wrong path or that he hasn't seen a thing properly or felt it properly. I don't do too much of that, because I have sympathetic and very advanced people who are budding artists. That's what I'm interested in. And the other side of it, which is much more elevated, is to have the student admit that he might relate the subject at hand to literature or to films or music or anything else that's much larger. I sometimes just play with ideas that have nothing to do with the matter, in order to stimulate an interest. I would talk, let's say, about the relation, and illustrate it, between some great piece of writing and photography. There's no book that's not full of photography. James Joyce is. Henry James is. That's a pet subject of mine, how those men are unconscious photographers.

In what way?
In the way they see.

Their imagery?
Yes. Joyce was one of the first. As you know, in *Ulysses* he was one of the first realists, and simple direct kind of man, whose language—he was partly a reporter. Photography is reporting, too.

You say that reporting and journalism are not good and that portraiture is a problem. There are so many problems, one wonders...
There are. I'm interested in reporting, but I think that reporting at its worst is journalism. But Hemingway was a hell of a good reporter, did it to begin with, and was always grounded in that.

Would you describe what makes a good photograph?
Detachment, lack of sentimentality, originality. A lot of things that sound rather empty, but I know what they mean. Let's say "visual impact." It may not mean much to anybody, but I could point it out. It's a quality that something has or does not have. Coherence. Some things are weak, some things are strong. If you've got something in front of you and you've got some students, you throw those words around and point things out.

What would visual impact be?
I purposely used it because it is a vague phrase. To me there are varying degrees of that in a picture. Sometimes it may be that that isn't the quality you want. I can show you a picture that's strong in it and one that's weak in it. A man interested in theater may say, "That isn't theater," or "that isn't good theater." I often say that in photography. Or that it's too pictorial. That's another thing I'm against. Throw these words around to make your students interested, make them come alive.

Forty years ago when I was going around with a camera, I was doing some things that I thought were too plain to be works of art. I began to wonder. I knew I *wanted* to be an artist, but I wondered if I really *was* an artist. I was doing such ordinary things that *I* could feel the difference, but I didn't have any support. Most people would look and say, "Well, that's nothing. What did you do that for? That's just a wreck of a car or a wreck of a man. That's nothing. That isn't art." They don't say that anymore.

You've prevailed.
Yes, prevailed.

What do you think has happened? Did people look and look and look and finally see?
Oh, I think what happened was that I was working beyond my means, beyond myself. I didn't know that I was as valuable as I was. I was led to believe that artists are something like mediums, anyway, many of them. Many of them don't know what they're doing.

Is it that that drives them?
Yes. I'm an instance of that. And it's wonderful to think that such a thing is true.

Do you feel a change in your work, or a sense of continuity, or development? Or does it just keep happening?
It keeps happening. I don't think very much about it. I've reached a point now that when a body of my work is written about, I'm always amazed at what people read into it. I don't know that I trust people that write. But I'm glad to see it taken seriously.

Isamu Noguchi in his studio, photograph by Russell Lynes, 1968. (*Courtesy Russell Lynes and Russell Lynes Papers*, *Archives of American Art*, *Smithsonian Institution*, *Washington*, *D.C.*)

ISAMU NOGUCHI

6

Few artists have written an autobiography of such vitality and passionate candor as *A Sculptor's World*, 1968, by Isamu Noguchi. Confronted by this book, an interviewer must attempt to find new areas to explore, new biographical information to discover. The following excerpts are from a series of interviews begun in November 1973 at the artist's studio in Long Island City, continued at his New York apartment, and completed, again, at the studio.

Isamu Noguchi was born in Los Angeles in 1904 and lived in Japan from the age of two to fourteen, when he returned to America to continue his education. Upon completing high school, he expressed a desire to become an artist. A friend arranged an apprenticeship with Gutzon Borglum. This brief experience was followed by study at the Leonardo da Vinci School in New York.

In 1926 Noguchi visited an exhibition of the works of Constantin Brancusi at the Joseph Brummer Gallery and was transfixed by the artist's vision. When Noguchi was in Paris in 1927 on a Guggenheim grant, Robert McAlmon introduced him to Brancusi. He worked half-days with the sculptor and attended drawing classes at the Grande Chaumière and Colarossi academies. It was also in Paris, at the studio of Morris Kantor, that Noguchi made his only paintings. By 1929 he had returned to New York, which became his home.

While Noguchi's need to maintain contact with the world is demonstrated by his multiple interests—sculpture, theater, parks, playgrounds, gardens, furniture, architecture, lanterns, and, recently, massive public projects—he remains an intensely private person. Whether working in the theater's space, in stone, in paper, in clay, or in metal, the imprint of his persona is commandingly evident. Avoiding the momentary questions that consume contemporary criticism, he contends with the major problems of life. In confronting these aspects of humanity with imagination, skill, and compassion, he has produced one of the most important artistic statements of the twentieth century.

You made Playground *and* Mountain, *the first play piece, in...?*

In about 1933, having done more heads and so forth and being disgusted with doing heads, I had a desire to get into another realm, another dimension. I suppose it's the same thing that makes us go to the moon—a desire to get away. Though I was popular, you might say (I knew a lot of people), I was not satisfied. Maybe that's your lonely traveler who tries to walk away and attempts to look at the world in a different way. I did three things then. One was called *Monument to the Plow.* The idea was a pyramid on the plains with a plow at the end. I did the model. I still think it would be a good idea to make it.

It's marvelous when you think in terms of earth art concepts.

I was a little ahead of the times. Then I did the *Monument to Ben Franklin*, which came about because of the triangle in front of the Franklin Institute [Science Museum and Planetarium] in Philadelphia. I thought of making a monument to Franklin there. The third thing I made was *Play Mountain*, because I thought that a New York City block could be much better used as a playground if it were three dimensional and in the form of a room, where you could go inside and outside—a big play object. I had done a head of Murdock Pemberton, who took me over to Robert Moses with the idea. Moses just laughed his head off and more or less threw us out. That was the beginning of my experience with the New York City Parks Department. I have no use for them whatsoever.

There are so many shapes, articulations, and forms in the plan that it seems pivotal.

It's a key piece. It was purely instinctive. I think that occasionally there are pivotal pieces that are not preconceived, but accidental—circumstances coming together. I did another thing then, called *Musical Weather Vane*.

Wasn't it in about 1933 that your interest in playgrounds and gardens came about? How did that happen?

The playground—*Play Mountain*—was a precursor of other playgrounds. It also tied into topography. From that to other types of topographical work was a natural transition.

In terms of studio sculpture, as opposed to the larger, outdoor pieces, do you find that you alternate, or does one take all your time?

No, I shift. You feel lonely after a while, and you want to have contact. I work with architects, dancers, and so on, partly for the contact, partly for the experience of working in more space.

Though you continued to produce heads of people for years, you also designed the playground.

The question of making abstract art as such—I had a period of it in Europe because of Constantin Brancusi, but it didn't last very long. I suppose it must have had something to do with my American background—rather skeptical—and a tendency to think of it in a puritanical way, feeling a little bit that it was an indulgence. We always thought of art as an indulgence. The truth is that it was much more a personal idiosyncrasy; I looked upon it with a certain skepticism. I'm not saying that's good; I think it's bad. But this skepticism pervaded the atmosphere; after all, there weren't many people who could override it. My only way of overriding it was to find a reason for doing art other than that of art. It had to have a purpose. So it was in 1933, I think, when I did *Play Mountain* and *Monument to the Plow*. Those things had a purpose that was not art, and, in a sense, that's what gave me the right to do them. It's bad upbringing and a puritanical, intolerant attitude toward art. Maybe that sort of thing is what underlies the antiart aspect of

American art today. I may very well come from that. I did not go for abstraction *per se.* It was one of those European indulgences that I didn't equate with real invention or real progress or real anything. Everything I did, therefore, outside of just doing heads for a long time, had to have a very definite excuse. My sort of leftist leanings precluded my doing anything other than that. For instance, I used to think of Sandy Calder as terribly reactionary. It turns out now that he's more liberal than I am. But in those days I used to regard him as just a plaything of the rich, while I was on the side of the downtrodden.

There are a number of artists who make art but don't want to be called artists.

Not only that, there are people selling as art that which is not art. I would say that I also occupy myself somewhat with art that, in a sense, is not definable as art as such. For example, the lanterns or playgrounds or parks. There's still a streak of suspicion and ill will toward calling something art and thereby getting away with it.

How did you begin designing the lanterns and the furniture?

I thought it a more honorable way of making a living, and I needed money also. It's part of the same kind of motivation. You know the American idea—every American is an inventor, in a sense. After all, that's how America was made, by invention—a screwdriver, a gear, or what-have-you. I recently did a nozzle for the fountain I'm doing in Detroit. It's a real invention. That sort of thing pleases me a lot. We Americans admire people like Alexander Graham Bell. They are the real artists of America.

Over the years your interest in a great variety of materials–bronze, clay, paper, wood, marble, aluminum–has become apparent. Do you still look for new materials?

No. It's a question of immediate convenience and what you can do with the material. I think materials limit you to that which you can do best. When you run out of the means that a certain material allows you and you want an effect that that material will not allow you, then you have to go on to another material. As a sculptor I always try to expand the possibility of sculpture. Being tied to one material limits me. It's like being tied to a style or to a certain technique. You're limited. You can't do more.

Then for you, sculpture encompasses anything and everything?
Yes. For instance, if Mark Rothko hadn't been tied to his brush, or whatever he happened to use, he could have had a new life and started all over again.

Some years ago you had an exhibition of balsa wood pieces; they turned up later cast in bronze.
I couldn't sell any balsa wood.

Why? People didn't believe in it as a material?
Yes, that's true. Same with the aluminum pieces. I tried to show them at the Stable Gallery in 1958, and Mrs. Eleanor Ward

View of Isamu Noguchi's studio, photograph by Russell Lynes, 1968. (*Courtesy Russell Lynes and Russell Lynes Papers, Archives of American Art, Smithsonian Institution, Washington, D.C.*)

didn't want them; she said they were too commercial looking, that they wouldn't sell. So I finished the marble pieces and had a marble show and didn't have the aluminum show until two years later, in 1961, at the Cordier & Ekstrom Gallery. Now, of course, everybody does aluminum things. But it takes time. It's no good to be ahead of the times. In fact, most of my sculptures today I don't show until—I wait as long as possible. The tendency has been, for very good and economic reasons, to call art that which was not called art before. These categories—these names—have become sort of blurred, purposely blurred; and it sells better as art, let's say, with a fancy price. I have a tendency to do exactly the opposite. I don't call my work art, I call it something else—a chair; even if it doesn't function very well as a chair, it's a chair. It's part of my orneriness not to want to ride on the coattails of art.

A lot of people have picked up Marcel Duchamp's idea of selecting an object and calling it art as an excuse.

Sure, sure, sure. The man who made the bicycle was a genius. The man who put the bicycle wheel on a pedestal is another kind of genius. He recognized that the man who invented the bicycle had neglected to consider that it might be a work of art. So long as it's useful it's lacking in that quality of art. When it becomes useless it becomes art. For instance, this thing here, this lantern—this *akari*—if it didn't have an electric light bulb in it, it could be mistaken for art. The very fact that you have a bulb in it removes it from the realm of art.

So thousands of people who have lanterns almost have a work of art?

Exactly.

When the light bulb is out it's a work of art.

Exactly.

To change the subject, was the Associated Press Building project at Rockefeller Center the largest stainless-steel sculpture made up to that point?

Yes.

Why was stainless steel chosen?

I've always had a suspicion about bronze, because things that are made in bronze immediately become art. In fact, doing my balsa things in bronze made them into art and therefore salable. In balsa wood, they were not yet art. Bronze smells of art; it's an official art material. Therefore, I had a kind of distaste for it, though I used to do a lot of bronze heads. I'm not saying that I haven't touched it. I have. But given the opportunity and the choice...

I did the Rockefeller Center sculpture in stainless and did the electrowelding of the sand pits and the grinding. It was an experiment, and, as such, the price of casting was negotiated down to being not too much more than bronze. It's in nine pieces and each piece is bigger than anything that had ever been done before. There are nine tons of stainless steel. You know, Brancusi wanted to have his *Endless Column* cast in stainless steel, but they could never figure out how to get somebody to pay for it. It would have been fabulous. I still think it should be done.

You did some of your best work during those years in your MacDougal Alley studio.

Yes. In that studio I felt guiltless for the first time. The war had freed me from any cause other than art. During the 1930s, there was in America, especially in New York, a sense almost of indecency that one could be occupied with art without some noble, moral cause behind it. This took various forms; it had political connotations. For a sculptor, it meant having to do direct carving. William Zorach absolutely foiled young aspiring artists before they could get started by saying, "It has to be directly carved." If it wasn't directly carved, you were just a son-of-a-bitch.

But you were never particularly influenced by that, were you?

Oh, yes, everybody was. They learned in school to do things in clay, but clay was slightly unethical. First of all, you had to have the money to cast it. It's an indirect process, therefore it's already suspect. I imagine there was also a reaction against Auguste Rodin. The Americans on the WPA, for instance, were trying to be American rather than European. You had to use American subject matter like the Hudson River School. And as for the influence of Alfred Stieglitz, John Marin, Charles Demuth, and Georgia O'Keeffe—they were thought of as an offshoot that didn't seem to jibe with the drive toward an American identity, whereas they now seem to be far more American for not trying for the local American scene. The American identity as art was very, very dubious. It was hung up on all sorts of social questions.

Was that because there was so little support for art in society generally?

Probably, yes. But mainly there was confusion. I never got on the WPA. And I objected very strongly when they wouldn't hire me. Of course, in a certain sense I have always had a sort of out-of-the-running kind of feeling. I still do. But now I have it with different groups. All this pop and funky business going on. I'm probably a little intolerant of it. I feel it's sort of a betrayal of art in many ways.

How is it a betrayal of art?

Because it doesn't go far enough. Those people take certain aspects of art and enlarge them to enormous proportions, then they think they've done something, when they haven't done a thing. They've just taken an aspect that existed and enlarged it, which is not serious enough. And those of us who are involved with a moral sense of trying to find the basis of any given art or material—for instance, if we worked with stone we wanted to find *that* stone, we weren't using stone for some other reason. And I still feel that way. So those of us who are, in a sense, wedded to the idea that an intrinsic quality resides in materials are suspicious when someone starts making things in an indirect way with materials, which, in themselves, are supposed to have the quality of being modern. I would say that *anything* is modern. The earth is modern, not old-fashioned; the ground is a modern medium. Of course, there are people now who have more or less come around to my point of view. They go out in the desert and dig a trench and say, "Look, we've found the earth." But to me that is a fragmentary thing. First of all, it's an artificial situation—the desert, let's say, so far away, like doing something on the moon. You don't have to go to the moon to do something. You can do it right here. When you give yourself special situations like that, it's a denial or an avoidance of the real problem. Though I rather like some of the things that are done out in the desert or some such place, it's just a little bit farfetched—an avoidance.

To go back to the mid 1940s, the war was on and...

I felt that if the world were to survive, sculpture had to be an important part of the living experience and not just something for collectors to buy.

So sculpture is a manifestation of your life and experience.

Yes. I wanted to know what sculpture could do in space, what it had done, what it was in time and place in former days, how it related to people's ceremonial view of life.

"Ceremonial?"

For instance, in plazas, and so forth, there was a ceremonial use of sculpture as effigies or temple plazas or dancing spots.

The general-on-the-horse kind of thing.

Marcus Aurelius on his horse in the Piazza del Campidoglio in Rome still has a great deal of significance. And of course when sculpture is used for religious purposes, it's very ceremonial; it has real significance. With the demise of religious art, art became a sort of self-perpetuating, self-regenerative thing. But to me that was not enough. There was no link to the general populace. Maybe there was to special, aesthetic groups, but I wished to find a relationship a little bit larger than that.

What do you mean by a regeneration of art by art?

Though I had a period of Brancusi that should have made me accept art—and I do accept art in its most aesthetically pure form, that is, without any reference to social issues—there is a kind of relationship that has nothing to do with a message. It has to do with people's places in the world, their sense of belonging. I think that kind of thing can be suggested by art. The whole business of measurement, of place, of situation, of how we function on the earth, and so forth, is extremely interesting to me. Of course, my association with Buckminster Fuller probably also influenced my feeling for geometry in the possibilities of art. That it's not just a personal whim; it's determined by the stars, so to speak. You are limited, of course: you limit yourself, which I think is rather good, because when you are unlimited you have no end. I remember Martha Graham used to say that in dancing she never opens her hand *out*, she closes it *in*, and this retains the energy. It doesn't flow out indiscriminately, it flows back into her.

Art that comes from art is limited by the very fact that somebody else has done it, that is, originally. Well, if you are able to circumvent that, you might find something. Also, I am very suspicious about your own influence upon yourself. If you are constantly reminded of what you have done and what you stand for, you become a stylist, blinded to larger possibilities. I think we all have a tendency as we go along to become more and more ourselves, in that sense. But it's not necessarily true that you're becoming more and more yourself. You do things that are similar to what you've done before. To break away is very important, because then you suddenly find that the things you thought were yourself may not necessarily be, and the fact that you trip yourself up and fall on your face gives you a chance to get up again and shake your head. For instance, I break a rock. I've damaged it. Then I try to make amends, and during the process I have a kind of dialogue with that stone. That sort of thing would be quite impossible to do in New York City. First of all, the material and the dialogue that I might have with the material would be of a different sort—would have to be. If I functioned more in the city, I would probably find the means of having a dialogue with whatever I find around me. I might very well go looking for junk, because that's what's here. The reason I haven't done it is because I think our present junk is too timely; that is, it's subject to decomposition. Maybe that's what makes it modern. But in dealing with stone you are, in a way, dealing outside of time. And you can take all the time in the world, because there's no grand rush to show it; nobody is waiting for you. Most of my things take years to do. I might say, "Well, I haven't got that much time. Why don't I cash in or capitalize on what I can perceive, instead of doing them and burying them, more or less?" Which is what I do. I'd like to show them, but it's awfully difficult. First of all, they're heavy. They're not likely to sell. Who wants to show them and why? The galleries haven't got the capacity to exhibit them. And what museum has that kind of dough? So you might say I'm sort of committing suicide in a way. However, I do it for my pleasure. That's the only reason I can give. I can't say that I'm so historically oriented as to think of myself in historical terms. I'd rather not. But I do think it's because it's essentially sculpture. And if I'm looking for sculpture, instead of crushing an automobile body, I'll crush stone. I don't deny that an automobile fender or something like that could be a medium of sculpture. Maybe I don't do anything so differently after all. But if I succeed, I have transcended not just our time, but all time. In fact, I am associated with all sculpture from the beginning of time. Like these granite things here. You can compare them to Stonehenge and see that they have more or less the same line. And one might ask, "Well, what's your identity then? Is it Japan? Is it New York? What is it? Why are you in New York?"

What you do in Italy is somewhat different.

Yes. However, I claim that I'm not that simple, that I'm all of these things, that I'm a person of the Stone Age and a person of this age, and for my real self to be apparent, it has to be looked at from various aspects. Even the paper things I've been doing relate me to lightness as opposed to weight, relate me more to people because they are consumable things.

In art one does not work isolated from humanity. My own areas of contact are not that broad. With these lanterns I have contact. With the plazas I have contact. With the stone things I don't have too much contact, except that they derive from my interest in landscape. I probably wouldn't be working in stone if I hadn't used stone in landscape. It's one of the natural mediums to use.

When you talk about materials (to go back to Zorach again and the truth to materials), in the 1930s one looked at a rock and saw the image indicated by the natural shape of the rock. But you've always seen such a different thing.

Well, Zorach could look into a rock and see a woman. I tried to look into a rock and *find* a rock, or at least the spirit of a rock, or maybe some relationship to human feelings in terms of the rock. It's not that easy.

Installation view of the exhibition *Isamu Noguchi*, 17 April–16 June 1968, The Whitney Museum of American Art. (*Courtesy of The Whitney Museum of American Art, New York)*

In the 1940s you used slate–thin sheets of stone.

I did those things in stone (I did them in wood originally, but I wasn't satisfied with the wood) because there were marble yards downtown being demolished for the development of Stuyvesant Town. The stone yards were completely demolished, and the stone could be gotten awfully cheaply. So [now] it becomes rather absurd to be using stone here; it's much more reasonable to do it in Italy. Or, if you're going to work in granite, do it in Japan.

They're accustomed to working with it?

Yes, and it's much easier. Occasionally I still do things in a flat material, but I tend more and more to do things in natural shapes. Though I think I feel that materials should be broken down into their components in order to handle them, in the sense that things are constructed of volumes, planes, and so forth, and the more you are able to segregate the various functions within the material, the more you are able to control it. For instance, breaking that rock gives me a toehold, so I'm using the rock totally instead of just tickling the surface. I'm within it. I don't necessarily break the rock, but I want to delve into it. That kind of attitude is quite different from, say, Bill Zorach's, who is trying to find a woman in it.

But no matter what the material, you seem to have a large vocabulary of shapes.

More than just a vocabulary of shapes, I'm interested in utilizing the natural forces inherent in that material from which the shapes derive. With metal, for instance, you can weld it, you can cut it, you can bend it, but when you want a complex curve it's not very clever to start off with a flat sheet, because you're up against it. You've got to hammer it into shape or whatever and then cast it. Then it's no longer the metal sheet that you were working with. Every medium has its limits. Stone is one of the more flexible ones. You can make a flat plane or you can make a curve.

Clay is also very flexible.

Clay is too flexible. There are no limits. Without limits the medium isn't really giving you anything at all, except a certain muddiness. But that muddiness is intrinsic. Well, we all come from mud so there is no doubt that it is an intrinsic form. But when you try to make the mud expressive, it congeals in some way. It's most often put into bronze, because clay won't last. I much prefer to make something in clay and bake it. And I've done ceramic sculptures. To me that's more honest, more direct. Not only that, clay goes through a transformation in the fire and acquires a new quality.

But one that is basically cast.

Which is intrinsic to it, you see. Making a thing in clay, casting it in plaster, making it in bronze, or whatever, or copying it in stone is a very roundabout, dishonest way of doing things.

Which leads me to the pointing machine, which you mention in your autobiography.

Yes. I made a few heads with it originally because it's the easiest way to get resemblance. You learn that way. But I don't use it any more. That was before I started doing these sheet stone pieces in 1945.

Is it the material that suggests ideas or projects to you?

When I'm working by myself without any program that I'm obliged to fill, I tend to be very concerned with material. Even when I do a project, I consider what material to use, what is feasible, economically and otherwise. You know, my capacities are not infinite. Though I might look that way, I'm not.

Well, let us think you are. How do you relate what you were doing in your studio to the problems that were set by the dance as envisioned by Martha Graham?

The theater stage was a challenging and basic concept. The volume of the stage and how things related within it and to the people moving was a sculptural problem. I think most of my efforts with gardens and so forth derive from my theatrical experience. They are the same thing—a given space demanding the creation of dramatic situations.

But did you think of the shapes for the stage in terms of sculpture, or as a particular solution to a problem—a prop that somebody would lean on or sit on?

Martha and others would tell me what was required. Martha would say, "I need a bed, an action that takes place on a bed." So I'd make a bed, more or less, very primitive, but still . . . I prefer to have requirements in a sense. If I'm left completely alone, I'm a little bit at sea. I enjoy a problem.

I was interested in the relationship of movement and space—how they interrelate. To me, just to do a sculpture and plunk it down really doesn't mean much. What sculpture? What shape? In that sense, I don't think I like sculpture very much. But when it becomes such an integral part that you no longer are conscious of it as a sculpture, then I think it's good.

What do you think of a small object as a work of art–as an object of contemplation?

Oh, I do those, too. It isn't that I disdain them. It's just that I worry about their ultimate purpose so far as the general life on this earth is concerned. It depends so much on museums—how it's related to the museum and the collector and so on. It's a dubious sort of outlet for art, I think. I would rather not know where my things go. I don't have much faith in myself as a kind of object maker with a sure audience. My audience, I'm afraid, is—I think it might develop after I'm dead, like Brancusi's, in a way. I don't think Brancusi had much of an audience when he was alive. I'm afraid that a lot of the prejudices that I blamed Brancusi for I can apply to myself. Though he wasn't interested in doing things because they were useful. I think usefulness is a kind of security of validity. If a thing is useful, people will use it and cherism it at least for the duration of its usefulness.

It's the idea of being consumed.

Yes. I once heard a talk by Marcel Duchamp in which he said more or less the same thing—that art is consumed. He said that his *Nude Descending a Staircase* was practically a hollow shell by now, because it has been overconsumed and was no longer useful. Those lanterns that I'm very much interested in right now—I've been making them for over twenty years. They have a usefulness, a life span of maybe a year or two.

You have a foundation named after them.

Yes. My idea was that after I went I wouldn't like this to just stop. I'd like it to keep on going, for a while, anyway. If a thing is a living tradition it should live; that is, its usefulness should continue. Last night I was talking with Christo. He packages objects or air or something else. I'm merely packaging light.

Do you think in terms of a form that will be illuminated from the inside and will have the shape of light?

No, the illumination travels from whatever source there is inside to the surface, so the whole surface becomes luminous. It's translucent light, not reflected light. Most objects you see are reflected light. Sculptures are all reflective objects. The lanterns are translucent and therefore have a somewhat different quality. To me, light in one of these paper bags is equivalent to gold—like crinkled gold sheets. I'd like to make *akari* so that people could get inside them. I think this sort of thing comes from my recollection of Japan and the *shoji* [screens] and the light coming from outside inside, so eventually you end up inside the light. I think I have that kind of feeling about sculpture, of wanting to be inside the sculpture. That's when you're really part of it. The usefulness is integral. In that sense, you can say that architecture is sculpture. I think of sculpture as something to be completely experienced, not just looked at. You're encased in it—a back-in-your-mother's-womb sort of thing. You're an integral part of it. Your environment is your sculpture, your world. It's *the* world, and the world then becomes a sculpture. So everything is sculpture. I think I'm a megalomaniac.

You've talked about Zorach and his "truth to the materials." One gets a greater sense of stone in the way you use materials than one gets from most other sculptors.

As I said, I have regard for the material. To me the excellence of sculpture derives very much from the material, the truth of the material. I feel that with stone it's possible to know what its truth is, because it's a part of our experience of this earth; we walk upon it. It's a part of our environment that is absolutely true. I don't feel that way about plastic, for example, because it's a strange and new medium. I don't know that plastic has any intrinsic character of its own. It may be a sort of gummy substance; you cannot break it open and say that it reveals itself. It's just a mess. If you break a piece of stone, it's stone revealed. And if you polish it, another quality is revealed. The medium is the message. But my medium is that with which I'm familiar and with which I associate the qualities of stone, of space, of the natural mediums—air, light, water.

So it goes back to basic, natural forces rather than to an imaginative source or the application of an idea to the material. It evolves from the material.

All our imagination derives from nature, and however we stretch it it alludes to things in nature. You take a geometric art such as Piet Mondrian's—it relates to nature and man's use of natural mediums. That's why he succeeds and others don't, because he had this link. You can see in his early drawings that he understood perfectly well. So when you say that I go to nature instead of to art—well, I think that when artists succeed it's because they have gone from nature to art, not from art to art. For instance, Arshile Gorky was enamored of Picasso and Joan Miró and so forth; he really didn't get very far away from them as prototypes. But when he went to Virginia and saw nature, he was suddenly aroused. I think young artists have a tendency to forget, to be unaware that they have to grow from some place.

It gives me great satisfaction to work with stone. It's something I can believe in. David Smith used to say, "Why don't you work with metal? Why don't you become a welder like me?" Well, for one thing I don't like working in a dark place with a flashing light, looking through a glass hood, with dirt and so on. It's not a medium that's friendly to me. I like working with wood or paper or stone, where you have a friendly relationship to the medium. But with metal—I'll do something in metal, yet, but it usually ends up with somebody else doing the welding for me. Stone is a direct medium. When you've finished with it, it's what you intended. It's not a translation. If you do something in bronze, for instance, you're actually doing something in clay or plastic or plaster or something, and somebody else reproduces it for you. It's a false, doubly-removed thing.

You've done some interesting projects in Japan. The memorial you did for your father at Keiō University, for example.

Well, in Japan, probably because of my childhood there, I want to be accepted, to be part of it. I'd like to be here, too, but I don't seem to get very far in New York City; I just don't get going. And I haven't succeeded in Japan either, for that matter. But when I went there in 1951, I did get involved with Hiroshima.

And the Hiroshima peace bridges.

And the bridges. I was given the opportunity to do it, because of a surge of interest in me at the time. I was even offered a memorial to the dead. It was rather farfetched after Americans had dropped the bomb to ask an American to do it. After I made the design, it was turned down by the committee. Probably because I was an American. But as an American I thought I'd do a little something.

You also did a garden for the Reader's Digest *in Japan.*

Yes, I was interested in gardens. They're one of the principal art enjoyments in Japan, especially for somebody who is a sculptor. Gardens are sculpture—the use of rocks and so forth. To get experience is very important; you can keep on looking at gardens or studying books about them, but to *do* a garden is very important. It's a more direct and public use.

Did you follow the style of the traditional Japanese gardens?

No, no. I was not particularly interested in the Japanese garden. First of all, it's too traditional. I wanted to be able to develop from that, to be free, and yet to be able to use the stones and so forth, use the materials available. Except for the UNESCO garden, where, in a sense, I felt obligated to do a somewhat Japanese garden, a kind of homage to Japan. So it's a Japanese garden and yet it's not a Japanese garden. I'd like to make a contemporary garden of stones.

Aren't the sculptures at Yale and at Chase Manhattan gardens?

Yes. To me, the one at Chase Manhattan is a contemporary garden. It may use rocks, but it's not a Japanese garden. It's different. Those two gardens are really wells; they're at the bottom of a kind of well. That's the sort of situation you wouldn't find in Japan. In that sense, they're not Japanese gardens at all. They relate to buildings that are very large compared to Japanese buildings. Japanese gardens are looked at from the inside of a low building, from a veranda, let's say, right out onto the garden. There's a kind of formal relationship.

You made some sheet-aluminum sculpture with Edison Price.

After doing the garden in Paris, I found working with stone impossible in New York. It just doesn't fit. You can bring stones here, but to work with them here is out of the question. The aluminum things came about through the particular machines that

Price had, that's all. I used a folding technique that may have come from *origami*, from folding paper in Japan as a child. It was a version of the structural use of stone that I had done before—I mean sheet stone. So you fold aluminum—they're derived from a single sheet of aluminum without any welding. They were interesting conceits on my part. There was no welding at all. You might say it's limited by what you are able to do out of a folded sheet of aluminum. You set your own limits. You set the limits of what a classical example of that sort of thing can do. The limits are inherent in the tools and the material. The same thing is true of a piece of marble; it's limited by the material and the technique available and what you wish to express.

When did you start gluing pieces of stone together?

Again, it's an extension of my structural use of stone. I used to do it by dovetailing sheet-stone things together. And I was interested in post-tension stone and made some columns with rods that you tighten up on either end so it holds together. From there you go on to piles of stone. I do a good deal of breaking of stone and putting it together. It's a kind of search for the structural relationship in the medium, not just leaving it alone, but shattering it, then putting it together again.

How do you break a huge stone?

You put wedges in it and shatter it, cleave it, break it. By breaking a thing you destroy it. The question is; How deliberately do you do it, and do you have a plan? And it usually works out that what you plan to do is not what you end up with, because the breakage has given it another character. By breaking it up, you enter inside the molecules, so to speak.

Can you control the break?

That's the point. It really doesn't matter; you might just as well break it any old place. I think and think and think and say, "All right, this is what I'm going to do." But if I did it any old place, it would probably do just as well. So I'm not liberated to that extent, but to the "indeterminacy of things," as John Cage would say. You might just as well do it by throwing dice. But why would you have to throw dice? You might just as well back into it and fall over.

It's a ritual, too.

All right, but you pretend that you have some control.

How do you handle a piece of many sections that has been sawed and carved and articulated?

Eventually, it becomes a kind of assemblage that you work on. It's like the walls of Machu Pichu. You don't suppose that those stones were just found like that? They were made that way. Why? Because they were crazy, that's all. It's a kind of madness you pursue for some reason or other. It has to fit. The result is your own private sort of pleasure. Things aren't done that way any more. There are people who are mad here too. They do things in their own way.

Fairfield Porter, photograph by Rudolph Burckhardt, ca. 1954–55. (*Courtesy Rudolph Burckhardt*)

FAIRFIELD PORTER

7

In the 1940's, when abstraction was becoming the dominant experience in American painting, Fairfield Porter (1907-1975) pursued the painting of traditional subject matter. His motifs—landscapes, interiors, still lifes, and occasionally, people—executed with vigorous, fully charged brush strokes, were set in an atmosphere filled with bursting light. Reflective, considered, yet often abrupt, Porter was schooled at Milton Academy, entered Harvard University at seventeen, and later studied at the Art Students League with Thomas Hart Benton (q.v.) and Boardman Robinson. He traveled in Europe, Russia, Scandinavia, Canada, and the United States, living at times in Illinois or New York, and finally in Southampton, Long Island. His summers were spent in Maine in a house, frequently represented in his paintings, that was built by his father, "a domestic architect." "In a sense," said Porter, "if I paint that house, I'm also painting a portrait of my father."

In this interview, conducted in Southampton on June 6 and 7, 1968, Porter discusses his education, writings, and several friends who influenced his thought. The artist taught briefly in 1936 at Rebel Arts, a socialist club formed in imitation of the John Reed Club, and thereafter intermittently at Queens College, Amherst College, the School of Visual Arts, and Long Island University. An occasional writer of poetry, he always retained an interest in words, and among his friends were many of the New York School poets. In the early 1940s, Porter provided illustrations for a book of John Wheelwright's poems.

In 1938, an exhibition in Chicago of Vuillard and Bonnard focused the young artist's ambition and direction. Though he never painted in the School of Paris mode, his images endorse a life of calm reflection. In 1939, when he left Chicago to again live in New York, through Walter Auerbach, he met Edwin Denby and, through Denby, the Willem de Koonings and Rudy Burkhardt. These encounters marked the beginning of his assimilation into the city's art milieu. In 1951 he began reviewing for *Art News*, where he remained until 1958, when he moved, for two years, to *The Nation*. That same year he began to exhibit at the Tibor de Nagy Gallery in New York. Though an avid student of art history, Porter felt he had "learned most as a painter from de Kooning, van Hooton, and Maroger, and [his] own contemporaries, Larry Rivers, Jane Freilicher, Alex Katz, John Button."

When did your interest in art begin?

Well, children like to draw, and I sort of stuck with it for some reason. I don't know why. I think I might have had literary interests, except that I read very slowly. I managed to do very well in school in spite of that.

When I was twelve, I was taken to the Chicago Art Institute by my mother, and I remember the first paintings that—I remember I always liked to see paintings. And the paintings I remember in the institute are Giovanni di Paolo's. The *Beheading of John the Baptist*, which was sort of fascinatingly gory. And Rockwell Kent I liked very much. And about that time, when I was twelve or thirteen, an exhibition of Pablo Picasso, the Egyptian period, those great big heads. That impressed me very much. I thought if this is what painting is, it's a significant activity. I copied Howard Pyle, and I copied photographs.

How would you evaluate the art education you received at Harvard?

I don't think I could have gotten a better education anywhere else at that time as far as history is concerned. But in aesthetics it was weak; there wasn't any relation to practice. It was theory, superficial theory. I found that out much, much later when I met

Willem de Kooning. First I thought I had found it out when I studied with Thomas Hart Benton. He seemed to go further. But then, when I met de Kooning, I thought Benton was not too deep.

Was there anyone there interested in modern art at that point–the late 1920s?

Arthur Pope. He explained cubism to us in an interesting way. Analytical cubism, he said, was like jazz. An intuitive remark, but I think it's true. And we were presented with the aesthetic theories of Bernard Berenson, which had a very strong influence on me. Even today, I look at Florentine painting in Berenson's terms.

I met him when I was in Italy in 1932. I remember telling him that I liked Tintoretto and Rubens, because I'd learned to like them from Thomas Benton. And Berenson said he knew what I meant about them, but the best painter of all was really Veronese, or Velázquez. At that time I didn't like either of them. But now I do. I think I like Velázquez better than any other painter.

When did you make that discovery?

After the last war, there was a show of the paintings from the Kaiser Friedrich Museum at the Metropolitan and there were some Velázquez *infantas*. I'd seen them before in Berlin. I was beginning to be interested in what you can do with paint—what is the quality of paint, what is its nature. And I admired the liquid surface of Velázquez. And what might be called his understatement, though I don't like that word. The impersonality—I don't know what word to use. He leaves things alone. It isn't that he copies nature; he doesn't impose himself upon it. He is open to it rather than wanting to twist it. Let the paint dictate to you. There's more there than there is in willful manipulation. I used to like Dostoevsky very, very, very much. Now I prefer Tolstoy for the same reason. He is like Velázquez for me.

What I like in painting—partly what I like in painting—is to rationalize what I like. The artist doesn't know what he knows in general; he only knows what he knows specifically. And what he knows in general or what *can* be known in general becomes apparent later, through what he has had to put down. That is to me the most interesting art form. You are not quite in control of nature; you are part of nature. It doesn't mean that you are helpless, either. It means that the whole question in art is to be wide awake, to be as attentive as possible, for the artist and for the person who looks at it or listens to it.

How did you like Boardman Robinson and Benton as instructors when you were at the Art Students League?

I liked Robinson best. He was a teacher. That is, he taught *you*, he didn't teach a system. He taught the person he was talking to. He never seemed to repeat himself. I listened to his criticisms as he went around the class. There were things he said again and again, but there was always something new. Whereas Benton presented the same system to everybody. And then you did it or not.

Robinson was a more interesting man than Benton. In life, too. He was interested in lots of things. He would bring ideas from the outside to the class. Benton's style as a man was to present a body

Installation view of the exhibition *Fairfield Porter's Maine*, 2–30 October 1977, Colby College Art Museum. (*Courtesy Colby College Art Museum, Waterville, Maine)*

of knowledge three feet long and three feet wide and one foot thick, and that was it. He had what James Truslow Adams calls the "mocker" pose. He liked to pretend; he liked to act as though he were the completely uneducated grandson of a crooked politician. I found that sort of tiresome.

There were life classes. There was drawing. Nobody taught painting. You could paint if you wanted to, but there wasn't anybody at the league who knew how to paint. None of the teachers did. I don't think anybody in America knew how to paint in oils at that time. Maybe John Sloan did. But he put it aside later on, didn't trust it. But there was something in American art at that time—the Armory Show was a complete disaster to American art, because it made people think that you *had* to do things in a certain style, and they gave up what they did in order to do this new thing. It was a little bit like selling whiskey to the Indians. A few painters got something from it, got a lot from it. John Marin got a lot from it. But American art was provincial before, and it became more provincial as a result of the Armory Show. Of course, there were people who were—provincial might mean dependent on somewhere else, or it might mean isolated from the world. In the latter sense, there were certainly very good painters in America. But they weren't in the mainstream.

Who would you say was in the mainstream in the 1920s?

Marin. The people Stieglitz showed. Benton. Kenneth Hayes Miller, I suppose, in this country. Sloan. And the illustrators of the American scene. They were naturally good painters—they had native talent, and they knew better than they thought. They didn't have any confidence. They couldn't keep on. They didn't know what to do next.

Was it at the league that you began to meet other painters and get involved in the art world in New York?

I met Marin in about 1938 or so, in New York. And I also met Paul Rosenfeld, who influenced me very much as a critic—his gift for language, for being able to describe what something was like, to put it into words. When I wrote criticism I was thinking of his criticism. Not just of Berenson. I remember things that Rosenfeld would say. I remember telling him I didn't like Odilon Redon, and Rosenfeld said, "What's the matter? Is he too ultraviolet?" And I thought that was exactly it! He had an impressionistic way of talking that was extremely accurate. Beautiful.

When did you start writing?

Not till after the war. I started writing art criticism. I got into it through Elaine de Kooning, who had been a reviewer on *Art News*. We went to a show at the Whitney Museum, a retrospective of Arshile Gorky. She talked to me about how good his things were. And I talked to her about how bad they were. We had a complete thorough disagreement about them. Apparently I expressed myself so well that, when she was leaving *Art News* and Tom Hess asked her who she could recommend as a reviewer, she recommended me. I jumped at the chance. I had always thought that I would be good at it, better than anybody. I had always thought that. And they liked me right away at *Art News*. As a matter of fact, Alfred Frankfurter, who was the editor-in-chief then, said, "He's so intense, I give him a year." I stayed for about seven years. And I could have kept on forever. Partly because I was painting, which would give me new ideas. You see, if you're not painting and you're a critic, you might get to an end and have to repeat yourself. I got ideas all the time for what I was doing, which renewed me.

So as the painting developed, the criticism would change and evolve.

Yes. And I'd go around to artists' studios and look at their work. The reason I was good was that my method was, I suppose, tentativeness. I would try as much as possible, when looking at something that I had to review, to cease to exist myself and simply identify with it, so that I could say something about it. I learned that because I was told to do it (not in those words) by my editors. Frankfurter said what I should do is just report, that the best criticism is simply the best description. And I think that is true.

I am somewhat in awe of any writer of poetry. I got in connection with the Tibor de Nagy Gallery, who published John O'Hara, John Ashbery, James Schuyler, and Kenneth Koch, through Larry Rivers's and Jane Freilicher's and Bill and Elaine de Kooning's recommendations. After I had been writing for *Art*

News for a few months, I wrote a review of one of the gallery's first shows. I thought it was the liveliest gallery in New York. That it was the place I would like to be in. So I got just exactly what I wanted.

I got in the Tibor de Nagy Gallery in 1951. They gave me a show. It was some new pictures and some old pictures, and it was kind of scrappy. But people were interested—I think because it was realistic and realistic in a different way from what they were used to. And artists were interested. They kept coming to those shows. They'd ask abstract artists like Jack Tworkov if there were any realist artists there. And he'd answer, "Well, there's Fairfield Porter." Some of them accept me; some of the abstract expressionist painters do accept me. In a way, I feel more at home with them than I do with people who aggressively call themselves realists. I don't feel at home with them. I don't feel at home either with people who aggressively call themselves abstract, like the American Abstract Artists. I couldn't have any connection with them.

How did you like writing reviews?

Well, they saw what I wrote about, and Tom Hess would think of things for me to do. I had a feeling that I was typed as the person to write about American art. I think it was because I didn't like American art. I thought I didn't like it very much, so I was a little bit less enthusiastic. My reviews were more critical, maybe more interesting, for that reason. So they gave me John Singer Sargent to write about, a big show of Sargent in Boston. And George Bellows, whom I put down. But they wouldn't give me the people I really would have liked. They did give me Winslow Homer, whom I was glad to write about. And Marin, whom I still have a kind of filial feeling toward. I don't know how much I like his pictures, but I can't ever get over the memory of how much he meant to me at one time, so he could never mean nothing to me. As a painter. I didn't know him very well.

Do you think that reviewing had an effect on your painting?

Yes. It did have an effect on my painting. Not just writing, but looking at things. I would think about something that I was writing about, and then I would think: If this is the way, why are they doing such and such? Then I'd have a look at my own painting and think: Why am I doing this? Why can't I do it differently?

You were never an abstract painter, were you?

No. Oh, in the thirties Clement Greenberg of *Partisan Review* asked me to write something about Bill de Kooning for that magazine. That was in 1938 or 1939. And I did write something. Greenberg and Dwight McDonald liked it, but the other editors didn't. So it came back, though Greenberg said it was very good, better than he could do. He was polite. So I sent it to *Kenyon Review*. One reason I never became an abstract painter is I used to see Greenberg regularly and we always argued, we always disagreed. Everything one of us said, the other would say no to. He told me I was very conceited. I thought my opinions were as good as his or better. I introduced him to de Kooning (Greenberg was publicizing Pollock at that time), and he said to de Kooning (who was painting the women), "You can't paint this way nowadays." And I thought: Who the hell is he to say that? He said, "You can't paint figuratively today." And I thought: If that's what he says, I think I will do just exactly what he says I can't do. That's all I will do. I might have become an abstract painter except for that. Another reason I paint the way I do is that in 1938 in the Art Institute in Chicago there was an exhibition of Vuillard and Bonnard. I looked at the Vuillards and thought that maybe they were just a revelation of the obvious, and why did one think of doing anything else when it was so natural to do that. And Saul Steinberg once asked me at a party if I painted the way I did for political reasons. For a person who's a humorist what a question! So I said, "No, not at all." When Bill de Kooning was first influenced by modern art, it was Picasso whom he emulated. With me it was Vuillard.

Do you make a lot of drawings?

I draw, but they're for my own use for painting. I develop a drawing around a color because it's something to use. That's what

Geoffrey Clements

Fairfield Porter, *The Screen Porch*, oil on canvas, 79½″ x 79½″, 1964. Collection of The Whitney Museum of American Art, New York. Lawrence H. Bloedel Bequest.

I want to know when I look at a drawing. I want to use it for something that's going to be colored. So I give myself that information.

The drawings are studies for paintings?

They're studies for paintings, or they're not studies for paintings. I think some day I might make a painting, or I already have the painting in mind when I make drawings. But usually what I'm thinking of is a painting eventually.

I think I was always very influenced by people's ideas of what painting is, what's important in it. Maybe beginning with Berenson's aesthetic ideas. And then Benton.

How were the early paintings painted?

They were painted in that Benton manner. He said reality is a series of hollows and bumps. He had an elaborate technique that was completely worthless, I think. It had no sense, no sensuousness as far as the medium is concerned. After all, a painting is made of paint. Benton is one of those painters who seems to be trying to overcome that, as though that were an unfortunate drawback. I suppose I was thinking that what I had to do was to learn how to paint. And there wasn't anybody who could teach me. I just had to learn it. So I set about copying the way things looked, trying to get the concept of reality down. Franz Kline once told about a class he had. A lady said to him, "I don't know what to do with this painting." He said, "Well, where you see green put down green, where you see blue put down blue." And that is true. And it's very hard to do. He hasn't really explained anything, or he's explained everything. One or the other. Nothing or everything.

You've painted a number of interiors and landscapes.

What I think now is that it doesn't matter much what you do. What matters is the painting. And since a reference to reality is the easiest thing, you just take what's there. And then, whether you've made anything or not, you hope it's significant. Well, what is significant? What counts? It's where this aesthetic theory business comes in. What does one think of? For instance, I painted a view recently. A great big painting. And it's because I looked out a window and saw it as if for the first time, in a new way. I saw it as something integral. And so I put this down on canvas. I'm not quite satisfied with it. In a way I like it. It always comes out differently than you think. And I might as well do it all over again. Why don't I do that? That's like inspiration. Again, it interests me to do it. I would do it differently this time, I hope. It would have that "all-at-onceness." What I admire in Alex Katz's paintings is that they remind me of a first experience in nature, the first experience of seeing. And that interests me more than— expressionism doesn't interest me very much, expressionism as a problem. But visualness interests me very much. And it must be that "first timeness"—the world starts in this picture. *That's* what I'm interested in.

Elaine de Kooning came around and looked at a picture in the studio. She said that that picture interested her because she never in the world would have thought of painting it. That I took as a great compliment. What I like in Vuillard is that what he's doing seems to be ordinary, but the extraordinary is everywhere.

Do you think that painting is more of an emotional expression than an intellectual one?

No, I don't think it's more emotional or more intellectual. I think it's a way of making the connection between yourself and everything. You connect yourself to everything that includes yourself by the process of painting. And the person who looks at it gets it vicariously. If you follow music you vicariously live the composer's efforts.

Don't you think the person looking at a painting has an entirely different relationship to it than the person who's painted it?

For one thing they see something that the person who's painted it hasn't seen—that's very hard for him to see. They are communicated with. They see the person who has painted it and his emotions, which he, maybe, doesn't see. When they say they don't like such and such an art, what they don't like is something that is really there. It isn't something that's imagined. I don't like Andrew Wyeth's paintings, for instance. It would be very hard for me to say why. I think the reason is that there's something he communicates to me that is disagreeable to me—something from him that I dislike. In him. You see the painter, you see the artist in the work. Ad Reinhardt. People see his paintings at a show, and it makes them very angry very often. Well, Ad Reinhardt was an infuriating man. And he got that into his paintings.

But calculatedly so?

Right. That's what was infuriating. That calculation.

Kenneth Noland, photograph by Renate Ponsold, c. 1977. (*Courtesy Kenneth Noland and André Emmerich Gallery*, *New York*)

Picasso's is wedded to the way he used materials. Matisse's really has no particular specific meaning. It's there, but it's not something that you get an expressive kick out of. You do, but it's loosely subject matter.

One of the biggest difficulties that painters have to face is what to paint. Drawing, which is the Western tradition and is essential to cubism, began to be purged or eliminated from the making of pictures. I'm not talking about drawing in the sense that it carries allusion to something outside of the painting. In abstract expressionism it had to turn into gesture and only allude to some kind of symbolism or surreal or pretty subject matter.

Did you make drawings in Paris with Ossip Zadkine?

Yes, I drew then. I don't draw anymore.

Why did you stop?

Drawing is the practice of projecting images or proportions or designing. I would rather keep that need involved in handling the materials, in making the painting. I'd rather work directly in the actual size and materials of what I'm doing.

When did you get to know Morris Louis?

I'm not sure, but it was around 1953. There was a school forming in Washington called the Workshop Center of the Arts. One afternoon I got a call from Louis. He asked me what the situation was in Washington in regard to teaching. I think he had been asked to teach at the Workshop Center. Anyway, we discussed it. I had been asked to teach there, too. So we both got teaching jobs at the night school at about the same time. We became very good friends. I knew other artists in Washington, but I became a friend of Morris's mostly because our interest in art coincided. I felt an affinity with his preferences in art more than I did with most of the other artists I knew in Washington. We'd see each other, oh, two or three times a week, and we talked a lot. We were close friends for about the first two years, and then for about two or three years we didn't see each other at all. About a year and a half before he died, we became friends again and saw quite a bit of each other, but by that time I had moved to New York.

What kind of cultural life was going on in Washington? There weren't many painters around.

There were quite a few teaching at the American University: Bob Gates, Helene MacKenzie, and others. Bill Calfee in Washington did a lot almost single-handedly to keep an interest going in painting. He was a professional artist and head of the art department at the American University. For a long time, there were no commercial galleries that would show contemporary art in Washington. So artists *had* to get together. They were dispersed. It was very difficult to keep lines of communication open and information going. There was another man, Robin Bond, an Englishman who had taught at A. S. Neill's Summerhill school and later taught at the Institute of Contemporary Arts. He had a lot to do with developing interest in art and art education in Washington.

Could we go back to discussing Morris Louis and what you two found in common?

I think it's possible to get sensitive or intelligent, in certain kinds of ways, in isolation. When Morris and I met, we were both in that condition. When we began to compare notes, we found that we had a lot in common. Coming together—bringing your own imagination together with someone else's, someone who has been doing the same thing—is very fruitful. It's not extraordinary in painting or in art; I think it always happened. Friendships are formed that are very helpful. Painting buddies.

Would you describe the similar ideas that you and Louis had.

Morris was very interested in Jackson Pollock, and so was I. That was the first thing. He had arrived at this independently. I had arrived at it mostly through Clement Greenberg. There was idealism—personal idealism—involved. And checking and comparing and bringing other kinds of information to each other. We both liked Bob Motherwell's work, which was unique at that point.

When did you meet Greenberg?

At Black Mountain College in about 1950 or 1951, when he was there for a summer session. I found him a very interesting man right from the first. We've been good friends ever since.

How did all this develop in Washington?

I had to make a choice between staying in Washington, where I could make a living, or moving to New York and having to struggle. At that point, if I had had a chance to make a living in New York, I would have preferred to have been there. But I'm glad I wasn't. I think by having that distance we weren't so influenced by current fashions in art. It gave us some distance to reflect upon things happening in New York, which was the center.

Did Greenberg go to Washington frequently?

Yes. Starting from about 1953, he would come down two or three times a year. And I used to see him in New York. Every time I'd get a chance to go to New York, I would call him, and he would always invite me over or take me around to see pictures or take me out to parties. I got the benefit of his incredible perceptions about what was going on in art and what he knew. On one trip to New York I brought Morris with me to meet him. Through mutual interests and everything, there were friendships. Also David Smith used to go to Washington. He was a good friend of mine. David also knew Morris, and he would come down to talk about art with us. We talked with Clem about art. That was very, very valuable experience for us. I have been influenced by quite a few men in relation to art, Clem, primarily, and David Smith. And Robin Bond. He had come to the United States to lecture and to go into Reichian therapy. And through him I went into Reichian therapy. That was a big influence. It had a great significance in my life—on my work, in opening me up personally, opening up my perceptions and my feelings, and, as a consequence, what I do. It's made me able to look at more of the world and myself.

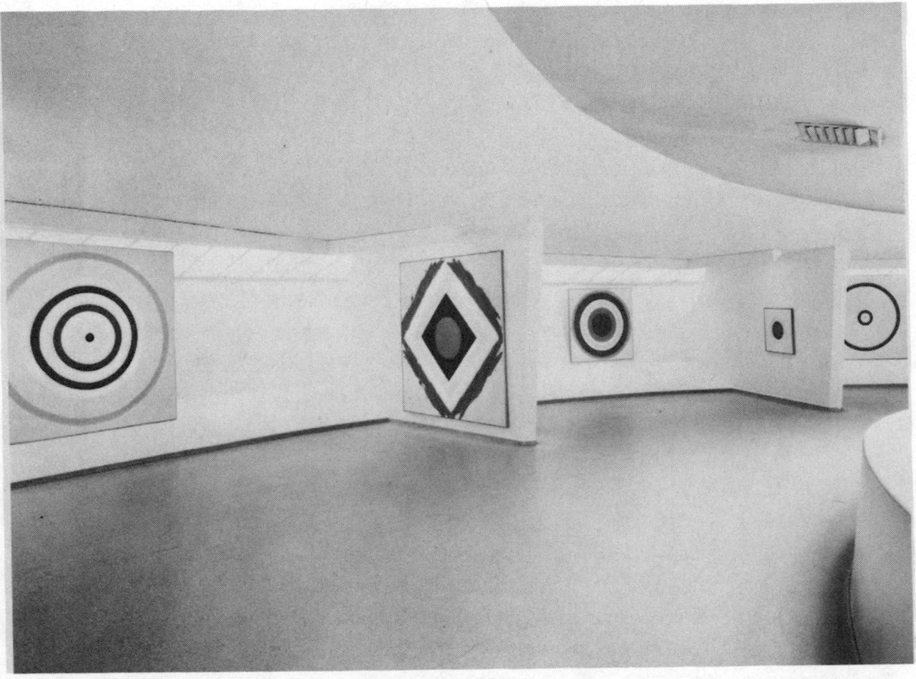

Robert E. Mates

Installation view of the exhibition *Kenneth Noland: A Retrospective*, 15 April–19 June 1977, The Solomon R. Guggenheim Museum. (*Courtesy The Solomon R. Guggenheim Museum, New York*)

Has it influenced the way you function–the amount of work you do, how you think about your work?

Yes. Without any doubt. It's been crucial to me.

It's a rather complicated kind of analysis. Why did you choose it?

Because it was undeniably true to me. I recognized the truth of what Wilhelm Reich was about.

It's interesting that you picked him over Freud or Jung, because in the fifties Reich wasn't really established.

At that time he was considered some kind of radical extremist. But the fact of the matter is that Reich's principles of life affirmation and life enhancement probably have more significance than almost any kind of work that's been done in the understanding of human beings, the functions of human beings.

I've found that it's very valuable for me to be able to check perceptions with others who take their perceptions seriously—who deal with their perceptions. It gives you the value of somebody else's insight into your own perceptions.

How does this relate to your work?

A lot that goes into making art obviously has to do with the way you feel about life—your experiences with life and with other people. Art is expressive in human terms, and one's experience with people and with life is somehow or other reflected in art.

May we discuss your painting for a while? In Paris, you were using oil paints, not acrylics. When did the shift in materials come?

That started in Washington. Morris had gotten Magna plastic paint from Leonard Bocour, because he was a friend of Bocour's. At that time Pollock was doing a lot of experimenting with materials. Part of it was out of necessity because artists couldn't afford to buy proper materials. It was just too damn expensive. And probably also because there's an urge in artists to use simple materials. This is a historical fact. Artists have always used very modest technology to produce art. Simple means and simple materials. There was other experimenting going on with materials. Pollock was using enamel. I'd experimented some, using dry pigments and making my own color. So the need for a new kind of material was always there, as it turned out, especially for color.

What about the shift into stain color?

It came through Pollock and from Pollock to Helen Frankenthaler and from Helen to Morris and me. Morris adapted it to his work first, I mean in relation to me. I was still experimenting with all different kinds of paints—that came from Pollock.

The concentric circles were done freehand, weren't they? Was tape involved?

No tape. They were painted by brush, freehand. I'd take a line and make a ring, but most all the edges were just drawn by eye and freehand.

In the stripe paintings you use tape.

Yes. It just made it simpler to use tape when I was making straight lines. I began to use it when I started making the horizontal stripe paintings. Up until then most of the chevrons were painted freehand or with rollers, but it was still freehand.

The concentric circles are so soft and the chevrons are so hard. Do you have a scheme that you follow?

When I begin to make a change from one kind of painting to another, I usually go back to very loose painting, fairly rough and fairly loose, in order to put it together, as it were, by hand. Then, as I get to a certain size or scale or spatial or tactile thing, I begin to set the process and get that sense of what those kinds of paintings are going to be.

Is that an unconscious activity?

Well, it is, and it isn't. What bothered me about the abstract expressionists, or about the way painting had been, was that painters had usually gotten set in a way of working. Morris and I talked about that. We figured that the best way to arrive at some way of making art that was more personal was to get into a process of changing. We found that this was different from Rothko and Newman and Still, because they had arrived at a way of making paintings that they kept doing. So that was a negative lesson we learned from abstract expressionism: to make changes and to learn to recognize not just to change from one picture to another, but, at some point, to throw everything into question and go back, to just rehandle the materials again.

Without some kind of preplanning, how do you decide what size to have a canvas? Or do you work in a freer way?

Oh, it's always based on a freer way, since I want to get at color. I believe in working quickly and simply to make a painting. So any way I can figure out how to do the work as easily as possible, to do more work, to get at the use of color, the use of material—art has to do with that, because if you've got more material to use and can devise ways of working with it more quickly, you can get at the sense of what you want to do.

Do you make a color study ahead of time?

No, I don't. It's all direct. I pick one after the other and go with it. I sometimes used to make color sketches.

But when you start, do you have any idea of what the proportions or the length or the height are going to be?

When you're dealing with the problem of proportions, which I do, and you know how many different parts you can use to make art, You can be fairly arbitrary about at what point you start. You can take any given size and let it set the conditions for other proportions in paintings. So it's not as if you have to plan it out. You're already in it, as it were.

The first choice sets up one point and the next and the next and the next?

Yes, if you're dealing with it constantly.

Even the selection of colors?

That would be included, too.

The same way?

Yes. You select colors on the same basis. It's based not so much on chance as on juggling, in a way. You handle simultaneously a lot of factors, such as opacity of color, transparency of color, tactility, sheer quantity, scale, size. You're dealing with all those things thrown up in the air. The final result is where you bring everything into a certain accordance: size, shape, coolness, warmth, density, transparency.

You can't change those colors once they're down, can you?

That's very difficult to do. If the painting fails, usually it fails on the basis of some color being too thin or too thick or too wide or too narrow, or the picture too long or too high, or the texture of the paint is wrong. And if you go back and try to change—put another color, cross color (which I do sometimes)—it's always difficult. And more than likely I fail at it more than I succeed, because I've changed the texture of the color all the way through, and that extra density of a second application of paint will throw the tactile balance out of whack. Or it will get too shiny or too matte or too rough, and then it'll jump out of the kind of balance that you've made. Space in my work, and color, especially spatial color, is changing all the time. That's really what it's about almost more than anything else.

Your vertical and horizontal lines seem to have a...

Yes, I know what you're talking about—a little optical illusion of depth. The early circles used to disturb people, because they looked like objects floating in a deep space. People aren't used to seeing that way. The white canvas looked as if it were just deep space. It was like an object hanging in the middle. At first they didn't like that. Like Morris Louis's narrow, vertical stripes just looked like columns at first. People used to wonder why he left the white canvas around them. I don't know whether these new pictures will ever look as flat as the early circles. I don't know. Different kinds of assertions go on in the new pictures in terms of the surface.

What started the new series?

It's very consistent with what I've been doing. I don't really feel it's that different. It's funny that the appearance of the pictures seems to make people think that they're different. I'm still dealing with the same things that I've been dealing with for a long time.

If we could recap a little and go back to Black Mountain and some of the people you had summer classes with–was Albers there?

He wasn't there much of the time that I was there. Actually, I studied with him for a half year. But I was very affected by the climate he created there.

He was head of the art department, wasn't he?

Yes, for a long time. He established the general climate there. I spent my studying time mostly with Bolotowsky. And there were other people who had a lot of effect on me. I studied music one summer. I've always had an interest in music. Not to the point where I wanted to be a musician or composer, but I learned a lot about it at Black Mountain.

Installation view of the exhibition *Kenneth Noland*, 10 December 1977–11 January 1978, André Emmerich Gallery. (*Courtesy André Emmerich Gallery, New York*)

Do you think music has influenced your thinking about paintings with regard to spacing and time?

Yes, as a matter of fact I do. You know, it's a little hard to associate it directly or reconcile it, but most all of the artists I know listen to music a lot. I think it probably has a great deal to do with some of the expressive quality that's in painting abstractly.

Figurative painting never interested you, did it? Was that because of Black Mountain?

Black Mountain College was a very advanced type of school, with Albers from the Bauhaus, and so on. Bolotowsky just took us back, as it were, as far as impressionism, when we were beginners, and through cubism into a kind of neoplastic abstract art and surrealism. So the education was fairly avant-garde. The figurative kind of art had already been, well, not thrown into question, but it had been developed toward abstraction by the cubists. It was just hanging around in semiabstract painting as what Clem Greenberg called "homeless representationalism." It was hanging around in abstract expressionism with a kind of very pretty subject matter. So it seemed that being able to make abstract painting had no reference to subject matter outside of itself, other than, say, an abstract kind of subject matter that had to do with space, concreteness, transparency, opacity, or whatever—a fairly pure way of experiencing nature.

In abstract painting there is some sense of the reality of the third dimension, in terms of spatial distances or coolness or warmth or concreteness or transparency, translucency, and so forth. Those are all different perceptual realities that get into painting in an emotionally expressive way.

You mentioned surface texture. Does the surface quality differ in tactile feeling because you use different paints?

In some cases. The difference in surface quality or tactility has always been as much a consideration for me in making paintings as the color itself, for you can't disassociate color from texture. Color is tactile. You can only describe colors in tactile terms—thinness and thickness, which are visually touchable factors. Transparency, opacity, matteness, dryness, sheens—those are all tactile terms. There are many different ways to apply paint. There is staining with rollers. I use a variety of ways of putting on paint depending upon the degree of thinness or thickness or matteness or sheen that I want the color to have.

It would depend on the viscosity of the liquid, too, wouldn't it?

Yes. That varies from color to color. All the different degrees. Some colors are buttery; some are as thin as water. All those ranges give you a difference of paint quality, give you a range of color.

Do you pick rollers because they make larger areas?

Yes. I can spread one color more uniformly across a distance of surface. The nature of the roller gives you a different dispersion of the paint in relation to the canvas.

You've never sprayed canvases, have you?

Yes. I had a spray gun in about 1957. I used it some in a couple of pictures, but I wasn't that interested in it.

From what you said it sounds like it's rather arbitrary, whether you paint a narrow, vertical painting or a wide, horizontal painting.

Well, it would be arbitrary in the sense of design. But in the sense of focus, it's not at all. Actually, different sizes, going anywhere from—I did a series of pictures that were six inches by eight feet, and pictures that were even thinner than that, or longer.

How did you divide them into that kind of proportion?

I had been working in smaller-sized pictures of extreme narrowness. I had one picture that seemed to have a very good proportion—six inches by eight feet—that offered the possibility of having a range of scales of color, or depth, going very deep in space to very shallow in space to very flat in space. The majority of the first circle paintings were six feet square. I'd made some that were five or seven or eight or nine or ten feet square. It was something that was physical to me, I guess. So at different points I locate an actual size that I will repeat, because I can extend many variances of scale or focus in that size.

So it is a natural selection rather than an intellectual problem?

No, it's not intellectual. The intellectual thing comes after the fact.

There are so many shapes. Were they done in a specific sequence?

There were chevron pictures that came before the diamond shapes. They were a step inbetween. Even though the pictures look different—circles, chevrons or diamonds, horizontal paintings, and so forth—I think generally the same preoccupations pertain in all the different kinds of pictures. And probably in all the different kinds of pictures that I make, I look for that possible range of size, scale, color possibility as a wide range. When you play back and forth between the arbitrariness and the strictness of the conditions of making pictures, it's a very delicate threshold.

You've said you don't plan the colors, that it's like juggling.

But you can plan the conditions for color. You can get together the references that will condition the use of color in relation to shape, to size, to focus, to depth, to tactility.

Have you developed a theory about the use of color, or is it an on-going experiment?

In working with color, which I guess has been my main impulse in painting, I've noticed that color has been used, and is constantly being used, as a means of communication. People see, make meaningful distinctions between colors. It's gradually beginning to be used as a way of understanding things. It turns out that the use of color is very important as a clear way of communicating distinctions between one thing and another. For instance, telephone and electric companies use different color codings. It's an easier way of understanding what goes where and what it does.

You've referred to space, either flat or shallow or deep. You don't seem to have a particular preference, or is it just not apparent?

I think it's important for people to be able to focus freely and emotionally on things that are both near and at a distance. I think that sheer visual perceptual feeling, which is emotional, should be opened up more. If you're depressed, sad, or whatever, your focus tends to be fuzzy. You might be able to look at surface details, but you don't see clearly at a great distance. Your vision is being emotionally affected. I think that opening up those different perceptual distances makes you able to perceive better emotionally.

Can you sense whether a painting's going to be a light painting or a dark painting, as far as feeling goes?

I can't sense it. I don't try to determine. I try very much not to determine what I might paint on any day, whether light or dark or warm or cool. I want the picture to come out of the experience, come out emotionally edited.

One gets the feeling that there's still a curious abstract expressionist freedom behind it all.

Yes.

It doesn't look like that, but your modus operandi was freed by the activities of the abstract expressionists.

Right. It was. Because there were two aspects of what they were doing. There was the aspect of the gestural freedom that developed. I think the gestural aspect turns into an intellectual development out of abstract expressionism, like pop art. But I think the handling of materials in an expressive sense, not a gesture sense, was a factor that was a little harder or a little different to get onto—being able to handle it loosely and stay in touch with the handling, rather than projecting some symbolic reference into it that was more intellectual.

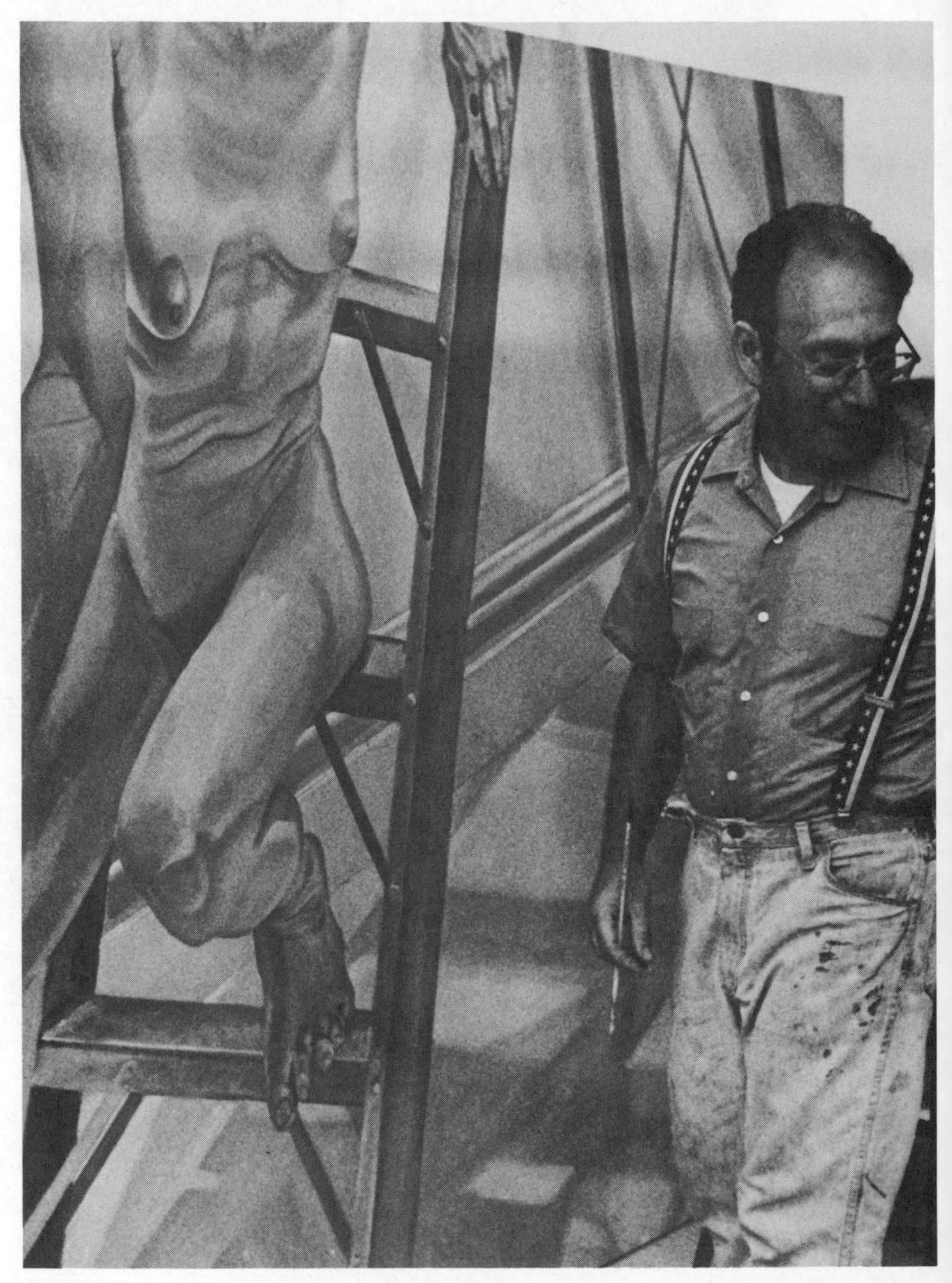

Philip Pearlstein in his studio, photograph by eeva-inkeri, June 1976. (*Courtesy Allan Frumkin Gallery, New York*)

PHILIP PEARLSTEIN

9

Rejecting certain modernist tendencies toward abstraction, though at the same time influenced by them, Philip Pearlstein has evolved a body of work using the figure as its central motif. Born in Pittsburgh in 1924, the artist studied at the Carnegie Institute of Technology and the Institute of Fine Arts, New York University. He taught at Pratt Institute and, since 1963, has been teaching at Brooklyn College.

In the early 1950s, when Pearlstein came to New York, the favored sources for young artists were the works of Jackson Pollock, Willem de Kooning, and Franz Kline. In his paintings of those years, Pearlstein adopted the painterly brush stroke of de Kooning, thus introducing abstract expressionist rhetoric into a new attitude toward figurative painting. (The modern American artist is often a contrary personality, functioning in society but espousing individual independence. This duality is so pervasive that only rarely do we find the organized artists' groups of influence or continuity so prevalent in Europe.)

Pearlstein studied art history as a possible career to support his painting. Informed by his professors that he would not be allowed to continue as both artist and art historian, he made his choice. He worked briefly at commercial art and later began teaching studio classes.

Throughout his career, Pearlstein has made drawings, a practice he continues at weekly sketch classes. The drawings from those classes become the source of his compositions. In his studio he restages the poses of different models, shifts the light, and paints. The process is described in the interview. Drawing is Pearlstein's source of renewal. Those who cease to draw are almost always hindered in the continued development of their art.

The interview was conducted in Pearlstein's studio in New York on June 8, and August 10, 1972.

Why did you want a Fulbright?

Well, it was like getting my M.A. at the Institute of Fine Arts—all the odds were against it. Nobody wanted me to have it. I remember a conversation I had with Carl Lehmann. I think I was the only one who got an A in his survey of Egyptian art. So he called me in, and we had a little chat: Was I studying Greek, and would I go off with him to Sante Fe? When I told him that I considered myself an artist, he said, "We have nothing more to say." And he never spoke to me again, not even to say hello. The same sort of thing with Walter Friedlander. He liked the paper I wrote, and we had a talk, and he asked, "Why are you here? Don't you know that we are the enemy of the artist?" So I stuck with it, just because "Screw you. If you don't want me, I'll do it anyway." So then I went on and did the thesis on Francis Picabia.

Now I want to get to when Picabia died. That was very important. I had my first one-man show at the Tanager. It got a very nice review from Robert Rosenblum, whom I had met at the institute. I didn't know him too well, just casually. When Picabia died, Rosenblum suggested to Hilton Kramer (who was then managing editor or something on *Arts* magazine) that they do an article, because I had all the material. In the meantime, Dorothy, my wife, suggested writing an article for *Art News*, a magazine that we were subscribing to. So I wrote to Tom Hess, and he asked me to submit an outline. Which I did. Which he rejected. But it was at this same period that Clement Greenberg had me in a show at the Kootz Gallery. I guess Hess was rather impressed when he saw me at the Kootz. He thought I was just a young art history student. After that he was always very friendly, though I don't think he's ever really liked my painting. I submitted the same outline to Kramer, who accepted it. It was rather important because it led to other articles in *Art News*, which really helped me define for myself the kind of painter I was.

Do you think that Picabia's ideas influenced you at the point you started researching his work?

What it did was get rid of modernism for me, because, having put so much time into it (it took me about two and a half years), I felt that I had paid my debt to society in terms of worrying about modern art. What I got was the idea that all that stuff is unimportant—that symbolism and all those dense intellectualizations have nothing to do with what is really good about art. The important thing is how it's done. So that's why I decided to concentrate on it.

What did you reject in avant-garde art–the theories or the art itself?

First of all, doing the thesis—I don't think it could have been done later, because too much has been published since on modern art. At that point, there was very little on cubism or anything. There were a couple of skinny little books on surrealism and almost nothing on futurism. One thing that did come out that was quite useful to me was Robert Motherwell's *The Dada Painters and Poets* [1951]. The only other readable or useful book on modern painting was the Skira survey [*History of Modern Painting*]—the first three volumes. I came across Daniel Kahnweiler's book on cubism [*The Rise of Cubism*, 1949], which has a marvelous section on Juan Gris, and Rosa Clough's doctoral dissertation in philosophy called *Looking Back on Futurism.* It's a terrific book. I got a lot out of it.

But it didn't take hold and ultimately you rejected modernism.

I reached a couple of decisions. One was that the subject matter had very little to do with the quality of the work, but that what it did do was set up a problem, and it was the way the artist solved the problem that gave the work its quality. The other was that all this modern stuff was as foreign to me as Florentine painting or Greek art. What went on in Paris in, say, 1910 had nothing at all to do with my life experience in Pittsburgh—culturally or visually.

Why burden yourself with having to follow somebody else's eccentricities?

Life in Pittsburgh wasn't like Paris.

No. And the people didn't look like Picassos. But I was influenced at that time by Willem de Kooning. The abstract expressionist thing was overblown. So I plunged right into that.

Did you ever paint nonfiguratively?

No. Because I also decided that I needed something to work from.

You've always had a model of some kind.

Yes. And rocks. I painted rocks for years. It was usually landscape or rocks. I was misusing abstract expressionism—using it as a kind of impressionism. That went on for the rest of the fifties.

You did large paintings with long strokes that had a landscape quality to them. I don't remember the colors.

Everybody commented on the color then. All abstract expressionism at that point was very muddy. At one point, it was almost like a black-and-white thing. So the color was—it came from the rocks. They were the source. It was a kind of naturalistic earth color.

Where did you find the rocks?

Dorothy and I spent a summer out at Montauk Point. I picked up a bunch of rocks on the beach, and that was what I painted from. As we moved from place to place, I carried a bushel basket of these rocks. They're still here, out in the back yard. They were my models.

What made you choose rocks as models?

First of all, I wasn't interested in describing the object as such. I was just looking for abstract compositions in nature. Also, everything about the abstract expressionist era had to do with nervousness, tenseness, frenetic . . . One day I picked up a rock. It looked very splintered. It looked neurotic to me. So I combed the beach looking for neurotic rocks. The summer after that we were up in Maine, on Deer Isle. There were big boulders—neurotic rocks with fractures. When the tide went out it looked like all these monsters had been stuck in the mud since prehistoric times. A sense of violence was there—the beginning of the world, that sort of thing. There were uprooted trees all over Deer Isle. I spent that summer making very, very meticulous line drawings of the huge root systems of these trees and of the fractured rocks. Then I painted from the drawings. I was bringing in all my skill as a mechanical draftsman.

Was this the standard way you worked then?

It was the beginning of it; I had never worked that way before. I got caught up in making these drawings. That summer I made about three dozen, spending a full day, if necessary, on each one. They were as carefully done and as realistic, as true to the object as I could make them. By eliminating the sky, by looking down instead of taking in the whole scene, I got a composition that was

Installation view of the exhibition *Philip Pearlstein: Paintings, Drawings, and Lithographs*, 20 September–8 November 1970, Georgia Museum of Art, The University of Georgia.*(Courtesy Philip Pearlstein)*

essentially a two-dimensional arrangement, and, at the same time, it corresponded to nature. When I went home I made paintings.

Do you still work that way?

Well, I made that series of drawings. I got back to New York and made abstract expressionist paintings, working from the drawings. When I had the Fulbright to Italy, I did the same thing there. I spent a year making drawings of the Roman Forum, Hadrian's Villa, and the Amalfi Drive. Those were all big nervous-looking rocks. But the idea, the symbolism, was still there in the back of my mind. These were all violent. Something violent had happened. The Roman ruins stand for something—a comment on civilization, if you will. But it was a kind of self-contained symbolism; it was there if you wanted it to be.

When I came back from Italy, I began drawing figures in Mercedes Matter's studio. The way she let the models pose, encouraged them to pose, looked to me just like the boulders in Maine. She saw that, too. I remember we talked about it. So it made a direct connection there. And I approached the drawing of figures in exactly the same way. The first ones were painted very freely, in somewhat abstract expressionist technique. I still make drawings like that, but now the paintings are also done from life in the same way.

So the drawings aren't necessarily studies for the paintings?

No. The drawings set up a situation that I'll duplicate when I come to do a painting. I'll work from a drawing.

The first show I had at the Frumkin in New York was the work that I had done from those Roman ruin drawings. It was extraordinarily disheartening, because the reviews weren't that great. Absolutely nothing sold. It was worse than any of the shows that I had had at Peridot. I guess that's when I made up my mind that it didn't matter what I did. So I switched to working from the figure right after that. But I was ready for that, anyway. I had been drawing from the figure for about a year at Mercedes Matter's studio. I knew that a lot of the drawings were as good as the drawings of the Roman ruins and would make good paintings. I had already begun trying to paint from them. I knew that showing the figures would mean a real cutoff of the past. I knew what the attitude was toward painting the figure strictly representationally.

Why did you choose Rome to go to on your Fulbright? Did you have a particular plan?

No. I was just going to continue painting landscapes and so forth, maybe more classical things. But I got involved in making the drawings instead.

Up to that point, what older artists had interested you?

Watteau. I guess I discovered Watteau and de Kooning about the same time. I saw the same things in them, only in Watteau they're in a miniature scale. But a little hand by Watteau has all the torment that a large de Kooning has or a Velázquez.

What about Chaim Soutine? Has he ever interested you?

Only in a peripheral sense. I think Soutine's success in America came after abstract expressionism. But everybody, including me, looked at him and late Monet through the eyes of the action painters.

Did you go to galleries and museums in Italy?

Oh, yes. A great deal. This time around I became much more interested in antiquity—Roman painting, Greek vase painting, Etruscan. And the Villa of the Mysteries was the great revelation of the year for me, though at that point I wasn't at all interested in figurative art. When I saw the villa, it just made Piero della Francesca look like a recapitulation.

What did it say to you?

What it said, very specifically, was that the gesture of the figure equals the picture composition. In the same way that Piranesi—I think what interested me in Piranesi (whom I began studying after I was involved in doing this stuff) was that his perspective system equalled the compositions. Exactly the same kind of thing the cubists did: scaffolding makes the composition. Cézanne's dots become a kind of composition.

When did you start collecting Piranesi prints?

When I discovered that you could buy them fairly cheaply.

Do you think they have influenced you?

No. I got involved with them after I had been through it. But the one lesson I've gotten from Piranesi, and which I use now, is that the perspective becomes part of the composition. It's not incidental to it or in opposition to it. The major lines that add up to, say, a Franz Kline-like movement happen to be going to a vanishing point. That was a real key to working with reality in terms of abstraction.

Do you paint landscapes now?

No. Since I decided to work only from direct observation, I haven't had a chance to do landscape.

What started your interest in the figure?

The original impetus came from Mercedes Matter. And her friend Charles Cajori started a sketch group. This was before I went to Italy. We would meet in somebody's loft. We met for about a year and a half, once a week; it was very casual. We hired models. We had a lot of things in common—the liking for Maine, for instance. Mercedes was the one who had told us about Deer Isle. That's how we got to draw the rocks up there. And when we were going to Italy, she spoke so ecstatically about the olive trees. There are implications of the figure in rocks, anyway. And in olive trees; they look like dancers. Another factor was that a lot of people began telling me that they saw figures in all these rock paintings. The ambiguity was one of the things that I wanted to get rid of.

Did you sense that, or was it a revelation when people would mention it?

It always came as a shock. Fortunately, I'd never hear about it until after the work was up and in an exhibition, and it was too late to worry. But I began looking for these things in the paintings as I did them, and whenever I spotted one, I would do my best to get rid of it.

When I came back from Italy, Mercedes had started a sketch group in her own studio. It had been going during the year I was away. This time it was a well-organized, very efficient group, at the beginning, anyway. Jack Tworkov came regularly for almost two years. George McNeil. Philip Guston came a couple of times. And Charles Cajori, Louis Finkelstein, Paul George, Mary Frank, Lois Dodd.

It sounds like the beginning of the Studio School.
It was, I think, though there was no direct connection.

The same kind of ambience.
And it was terrific. They would meet to draw for six hours in the evening. That was too much of a grind, so I'd come an hour late. But I found that very rough going. They'd change the pose every twenty minutes. Mercedes was always pressing for a longer period, and gradually they became forty minutes long, then sixty minutes long. Occasionally, one posed for the whole night. Anyway, the group slowly changed. Everybody worked totally independently. There was no discussion of each other's work or anything. It was a very exciting thing to be involved in. This went on and on, year after year, until gradually the personnel changed. But some of us are still there. We are still meeting once a week. About five years ago, it split into two groups. Because most of us teach, it became convenient for some to meet on Wednesday night, rather than Friday or Sunday night. I'm with the Sunday night group.

Where do you meet?
It's shifted around quite a bit. For a few years we met at Mercedes's place. She had a marvelous studio in MacDougal Alley, which was attached to the [original] Whitney. I don't know whether it's part of the Studio School now or not. Then she had a loft on Second Avenue for a time. After she left there, we met at Lois Dodd's loft for a few years. Then a sculptor named Bill White had us at his place for a while. Then back to Lois Dodd's place. For a couple of years we met at the Studio School on Sunday

nights. Then the students chased us out, and we met again at Lois Dodd's. They met at the studio of Sideo Fromboluti and his wife, Nora Speyer. Then back to Lois Dodd's studio. And then for two years we met first at my place and then at Louis Finkelstein's house.

Would you tell me about your exhibitions with Frumkin?

At first the going was very slow, especially after I made the switch from the expressionist landscape to the figure. The first figure things were expressionistic, but my intention was not expressionistic. And nobody took them as expressionistic. They saw them as very tightly painted realistic. Which is quite curious, now, because now they look very brushy and loose and full of emotion. But then they were talked about as being cool and reserved. The drawing show was at the end of the season. I guess it was what helped me get established as a figurative painter. That show was taken seriously. Out of it I got a teaching job at Yale, as visiting critic for the year. And I was invited to several museum shows. The drawing show was invited to the Kansas City Art Institute. And out of that eventually grew the Georgia Museum of Art retrospective, ten years later.

Do you still draw in the same way?

Yes, very, very close. Maybe the earlier drawings are a little more hesitant.

How did the broken line develop?

It was just a way of dealing fast with a problem. I usually start a drawing by making a few points to mark out the main things, like elbows, feet, and so forth. But I don't pay any attention to that after I start. I start wth one particular spot. The dotted line is a fast way of indicating a different kind of line. In other words, it's an interior contour line rather than a definitive hard-edge line, or a way of indicating where a shadow is going to fall. It's one of those things that meant something to me. I never thought they had a stylistic character, but everybody else saw them that way.

I work the drawing out in line first. My years as a professional mechanical draftsman conditioned a lot of this. I work it out in line, and then the wash goes on at the end, usually rather quickly, just to help establish the form at first. I've gotten more elaborate trying to establish atmosphere.

Are they all done with a brush?

Again, from my days of drafting, I use Japanese brushes, because they give you a very, very fine point, and they're very flexible. I just wasn't used to working with a pencil. And a pen gave too hard a line. Most of the landscape drawings were done in this wash. The drawings are very consistent.

What was it like, seeing your retrospective?

The overall effect was rather strange. You don't remember what you've been through. What intrigued me most, though, was that when I thought I had made an abrupt transition from the landscape to the figure and had turned my back on expressionism, it didn't show, because so many of the early figure paintings seemed to be a direct continuation of the landscapes. There wasn't the abrupt break that I had thought there was.

And, as you said, the figures grew out of the rocks.

Yes. In terms of color, paint-handling, and everything, it was a very easy transition.

What is the difference between the earlier expressionist works and the more recent, as you say, "cool" ones?

It has to do primarily with intent, but I think one laid the groundwork for the other. The expressionist period is essentially abstract, even though the motifs are taken from nature, and all the drawings I made were as accurate as I could make them. I was really concerned with abstract ideas in painting, how a painting is put together. That's what I've always been primarily interested in. That was my laboratory space. There were ideas from Zen—Chinese painting or Japanese painting—along with Cézanne, Piet Mondrian, the Renaissance—everything put together. I think it gave me an assurance about picture construction. But now that's all just intuitive. The figure has that built into it automatically.

eeva-inkeri

Philip Pearlstein, *Two Female Models Reclining on Cast Iron Bed*, oil on canvas, 72″ x 72″, 1976 (*Courtesy Allan Frumkin Gallery, New York*)

So there was one point when there was an obvious activity of building: What does this do? What does that do?

Yes. I think they relate much more to the Cézanne, cubist tradition.

What about Zen and Japanese painting? Where does that come in?

It came about through art history courses at the Institute of Fine Arts and studying Chinese landscape painting. I was studying it at about the same time that I was becoming aware of de Kooning and the abstract expressionists. And I really didn't see that much difference. When I was painting, I was almost using technical points from both.

Did you get involved with Oriental philosophy?
It wasn't Zen philosophy. Philosophy has never touched me from any source. The one thing that did come through, which I think I use now, is the idea of identification with the model—you become the thing in order to draw it. Well, you don't have to *become* it, but you certainly have to pay very close attention to it.

A kind of empathy.
Yes. The rest was all kind of technical. I could see the close relationship between what I understand Cézanne's technical points to be—I could see them in Chinese painting. I've never had the time to work it out or even to study Cézanne that thoroughly to find out whether he observed Chinese painting.

Were the early figurative paintings edited?
The drawings were.

You said the drawings preceded the paintings at one point.
Yes.

Does that continue?
Yes, it continues.

The drawings are still a little ahead?
No, no. That's not what I mean. I think for the last few years, for the first time in my creative life, I've felt the drawings were accessories to the paintings, not independent, not better than, not more successful. I've been using them mostly as a way of finding compositions. They're almost always done in somebody else's loft. Then I attempt to restage the models into a successful composition. But it never works; it always ends up being different—almost always. Very few of the drawings really relate to the final painting.

But a group of drawings could lead to one or two paintings?
Right.

But not this drawing to that painting.
Sometimes, but not often. Also the graphic work—the printmaking—has come out of the drawing activity, and in turn has influenced my drawing.

When did you start making prints?
In about 1967 or 1968. I was teaching at Pratt. They have a practice of inviting any artist teaching there to use their print facilities. So I did.

How do you like it? You've made a number now, so you must be interested.
The drawings have always been done very fast, without dwelling over them, without really taking as much time as one always feels one would like to take. So working with the lithograph crayon on a plate or on a stone, I feel free to spend as much time as I want. It's really been a self-indulgence that way, just to see how far I could take a drawing.

In what sense?
To develop it. How round the forms can become without getting overburdened with shape. How much atmosphere can be developed. And, as a result of that, I think, I recently got involved in using pencil for the first time. I had done pencil drawings before, but not to any great extent. I began using pencil in the Sunday night drawing trips, using a very soft lead pencil, thick, roughly the equivalent of a lithographic crayon. So it had that kind of influence. With a couple of prints I tried using a wash technique, which I thought would correspond very easily to my use of wash in the drawings. For me it did not come off well; they were too expressionistic looking. But they've been the most successful prints I've done. Two of them have really been very, very popular. And recently I've begun doing aquatint etchings. I started largely because Robert Birmelin told me one day that he thought I would probably do pretty well with etchings. So he gave

me a couple of zinc plates all ready to etch. I worked them out and then they were printed at Robert Blackburn's studio. They were fairly crude looking, but I could see possibilities.

Often you have two figures–two models–in one painting in very different juxtapositions, where the bodies seem to come out or down . . .

That comes partly out of Mercedes's habit, not habit—how she set up the models. Having more than one model was her idea. Of course, it increases the complexity. It makes it much more like a bunch of rocks lying around. If you get more than two, I find it becomes a problem in terms of subject matter. It gets out of hand. You have a party going on or a theatrical performance or something.

In what way?

We had three models a few times, and I guess it begins to dissipate the compositional energy, the compactness. Scale becomes smaller. To encompass three or more figures they all have to become somewhat smaller. I like to have them as big as possible. I guess that would be the main reason. But the other is a kind of implication of an orgy going on, or a bathhouse kind of thing. With two figures you may have implications of something, but at least it's intimate.

There seems to be a series of carpets that runs through your works.

That's a more recent thing. That corresponds with the printmaking activity. The first time I consciously used a rug as another element in design was in a lithograph I did in Florida. The University of South Florida in Tampa asked me down when they set up a print workshop. The model brought her own blanket. It had a couple of big bold stripes on it. Immediately I saw that it became an organizing factor. It helped enrich this black-and-white medium; it brought additional coloristic values.

Most of the time you've had a sofa or bed corner or something very bland.

Right. I've been using rugs more and more, partly because I've sort of fallen in love with them. I have almost as much respect for the rug as I have for the model. The rug really becomes part of the subject. In a sense, maybe, it takes the place of a third person. It increases the complexity, while allowing the big scale to remain. It gives you a sort of counterpoint effect. Also, it helps bring in a greater color range.

Your color has changed quite a bit over the years.

Yes, it has. That's partly because of the accessories—the rugs—and partly because I stopped using certain colors and gradually moved into another range of colors.

Why?

When I started the figures I just kept the same colors that I had had for the landscapes. Even then, I seemed to have a peculiar color range. I really liked Mars violet, Mars red, Mars black, cobalt violet, ultramarine violet, green earth; I was using that whole earth range of colors for the figures, at first. Then gradually those colors were eliminated. Mars violet, Mars red, Mars brown were among the first to go. Gradually, I've added other colors.

The flesh quality has become fleshier looking.

Each model comes with her own color. I just tried to work with the colors I saw. In order to do that I had to add colors. And some weren't usable, so I dropped them. Now there's more cadmium red light, Naples yellow—colors that I hadn't used before have come to dominate. Among others that I stopped using are cadmium yellow, burnt sienna, burnt umber. I use only raw umber and raw sienna.

How do you draw on the canvas?

With a brush, but linear. I'm primitive. I start filling in the color.

What kind of materials do you use?

I'll start the drawing usually with raw sienna or yellow or something that will disappear and become part of the painting immediately. Even charcoal won't work because it smears; you can't get rid of it. So I just paint with turpentine and very thin paint.

Carl Andre, *Prime Terrane*, dolomitic cement blocks, overall: 8″ x 36′ x 55′, 1976. Installation at The Detroit Institute of Arts, June 1976–May 1977. The artist stands at upper left. (*Courtesy Sperone Westwater Fischer, Inc., New York*)

How do you get the models' poses?

They take the poses themselves, usually. We start with, say, a drawing; the drawing might have been of other models, so it simply doesn't fit this one. I keep saying it's a kind of choreography, in a way. I mean, *I'm* not choreographing them. I'm just an observer watching movements, just appreciating their movements and freezing them.

How do you decide how much of the figure you'll include?

I don't worry about it. For me, what counts are the movements, the axial movement, the direction in which the forms move. So, if the torso is moving well, it doesn't need the head. If the head is moving in an altogether different way and I like it, I'll start with the head and let the feet go. It's how these things crisscross across the surface of the canvas that really matters.

It's almost an abstract concept, rather than a portrayal of the individual.

Right. It comes out of abstraction. And I hope that it's the abstract element that will give it its lasting power, rather than just the subject or description.

I don't know whether I've said it, but in a sense I got involved accidentally with the realist problem. I was dealing with the problems of movement, and a feeling of obligation to make it look more and more true to the model developed gradually. Becoming aware of all the problems developed gradually.

CARL ANDRE

10

Carl Andre, born in 1935 in Quincy, Massachusetts, an industrial suburb south of Boston, is a descendant of a family of craftsmen. His father worked as a professional draftsman in the Bethlehem Steel Shipbuilding Company, and his mother wrote poetry; so, soon, did Andre. The family was fascinated with words. Poetry was read aloud, and Andre remembers reading dictionaries, encyclopedias, technical books, and books on geometry. He visited the local museum with his father, coming to prefer three-dimensional objects to paintings. The quarries near Quincy, with "their drills, grinding machines, and slabs of granite and other stones," remain vivid images in his mind, as do the "steel plates and heavy industry of the shipyard."

In painting class at Phillips Andover Academy he responded to the physical manipulation of paint rather than to the formation of images. In 1956 he joined the army, serving in the intelligence services, often as an interrogator. He was demobilized three months early because he was accepted at Northeastern University. Living in Quincy, he attended college until his first G.I. Bill checks arrived, whereupon he left for New York. He worked for a year at Prentice-Hall as an editorial assistant, and, from 1960 to 1964, for the Pennsylvania Railroad.

Interviewed in September 1972 in his Westbeth studio in New York, Andre comments on the development of his attitudes toward sculpture, his seminal friendship with Hollis Frampton, and the importance of Frank Stella, with whom he shared studio space. "I once made a formulation, half in jest, that the three art influences were Patrick and Maude Morgan, who served as an in factor. They pointed out that art is actually produced. It's from human energy and not the energy of the dead, but the energy of the living. From Hollis—the sense of the ego energy. That is, that not only is it the living who produce art, it is we who produce art, ourselves who produce art. And then Frank—not only that we the living produce art, but we must establish what we're going to do and by what measures and standards."

Andre has moved away from the dramatic images of conflict that characterized much of the sculpture of the 1950s under the influence of abstract expressionism. He wishes to express "restfulness," a nonthreatening physicality stated through organization—space intruded upon or space definitively formed—and through industrially produced components. He is uninterested in the unique. "Sculpture," he says, "is a more primitive form than painting, the way poetry is a more primitive prose."

Who taught the studio classes at Andover?

Patrick Morgan was the artist in residence, the senior art presence. The junior art presence was Gordon Bensley.

Tell me about Patrick Morgan.

He had studied in Germany with Hans Hofmann, I think, before he came to America. His wife was also a painter. They were very interested in contemporary American art—Jackson Pollock and Franz Kline and Willem de Kooning—very much aware of it.

You came in on a very contemporary level. What classes did you have at Andover?

There was no instruction. If you wanted to draw something, fine, absolutely fine. If there was some technical matter that you wanted to know about, fine. The lecture course was pretty much a study of twentieth-century art.

Coming in with no background, did you like that system–just being told to do what you want?

It was glorious, because I liked the physical manipulation of materials—the paint, the brush, that type of thing. I never, never had an art talent or intention; I wasn't the kind of child who was artistically gifted or who draws Donald Duck. You know, "He's five years old and he can draw Donald Duck! Isn't that marvelous?"

Did you make drawings?

Never, never did. I still don't make drawings. I never had a drawing course in my life, and I can't draw. I can't even doodle decently.

I used to like to build things as a child. I've always been drawn toward mass and weight and three-dimensional stuff, not toward representation at all, or portrayal. The thing I liked about painting was actually pushing the pigments around—the physical aspects of the painting.

What students were particular friends of yours at school?

One of my two roommates the first year at Andover, the junior year, was Hollis Frampton. He was a year below me, but they had a policy of putting new boys together in a house smaller than the large dormitories, and Hollis and I immediately hit it off. Both of us wrote poetry. I wrote poetry before I got to Andover. It was quite a natural and enjoyable thing to do. But Hollis knew a great deal more about contemporary literature and avant-garde literature, not just in English either.

I met another friend of mine then, name of Michael Chapman, who is a professional movie cameraman now. He wasn't involved with film then. Hollis's involvement is very much more with avant-garde film. Michael was then a writer; he's still writing—screenplays. But he was a writer of short stories and essays then, as Hollis was. Michael also was into painting, very interesting representational paintings. But I was never involved with representation at all. I was really an abstract primitive. I just don't have a tradition of being involved as an artist in any kind of representational mode whatsoever.

What did you paint in your first classes at school?

I remember there was a still life of a couple of old army boots, really beat-up old boots, thc kind of perfect Vincent van Goghish subject. I gradually just brought the still life into sort of cloudlike shapes and suppressed all color except gray.

One thing I occasionally tried to do there, but didn't, was sculpture, because school was very painting oriented. I've never particularly liked modeling clay. I remember doing a painting once that had a plaster snake, three dimensional. There was always the urge of wanting to go into a three-dimensional space, but not going into a three-dimensional space by portrayal. I think during the summer and at home in Quincy, I did do sculpture, because my father was a carpenter and had a basement workshop. I remember, later on, cutting wood with a radial arm saw, but also chiseling. I can remember once doing a masklike face out of a large block of wood; that was a representational sculpture.

Was this in your second year at school?

It sort of goes into the second year. I can't distinguish. I remember there was *The Mirror*, which was the school literary magazine. Pieces of mine were accepted for that in my first year, and drawings and paintings were reproduced.

What were you writing?

Poems. Almost all poetry, really. They were all more or less experimental forms, or free verse, but again, in a kind of avant-garde primitive way, because I didn't know much about what was going on and what had gone on—none of the grand tradition of the avant-garde of Mallarmé and all that nonsense. I knew Edgar Allen Poe, so my origins were the same as Mallarmé and Paul Valéry's. A lot of critics can't understand what appeal Poe had for people, because he was such a hack, but I understand the appeal that he has for the French.

Poe insisted on an incredible beat to his poetry, too.

Yes, he uses—there was always a kind of mechanical engine working in Poe, disguising the complete irrationality of what he's talking about. Quite mad, but you don't realize it's mad because...

It explodes all over.

Yeah, exactly, exactly. And then, in my senior year at Andover, I took five studio hours a week and two lecture periods a week. The lectures were concerned with breaking down the attitude that art of one period was exclusive or better than or an improvement on art of another period. It was trying to find underlying principles that seemed to be constant through art.

Do you think those principles are there?

I think so, essentially. I think what underlies all art is that it's done *by* people *for* people, and people don't vary that much. Basic needs and desires don't vary that much. Of course, art will look different in different cultures, but it's not a forbidden thing to cross cultures at all, as we've done.

You found Andover exciting, rewarding?

Oh yes, indeed. I realized at Andover that art was done by the living for the living. It was a living and visual activity, not one that was suspect or that had to be dead in order to be appreciated or followed. It was my greatest pleasure. They couldn't pry me out of that studio. I found at the same time that any ambition in science was completely eliminated because science was something I found absolutely not gratifying. It was like the height of meticulous bookkeeping combined with recipe following. I just couldn't stand it. But still, to this day, I have a liking for the properties of science as opposed to quantities. The qualities of science still interest me, and I'm a regular reader of *Scientific American* and technical books and so forth. I've never been able to grasp the quantities of science, only the qualities.

Well, to finish up the Andover thing. Frank Stella was in the same class as Hollis and working in the studio at the same time I was in my senior year. I can remember working in the same studio with him, but not really knowing him. I remember the work he was doing. Sort of abstract expressionist brush studies on paper and so forth. I remember seeing at the time, in 1952 or 1953, a show of Franz Kline drawings in one of the galleries in Boston that were done on telephone directory pages.

So Frank was doing drawings of things like that. The kind of work I was doing was very much neoconstructivist—severe geometric postsynthetic cubism, neo-all-kinds-of-stuff—or kind of Paul Klee witticism stuff. I'm not saying it was like Klee, just in appearance, and I would say very—kind of geometric abstractions.

Were you interested in Piet Mondrian, De Stijl, and Theo Van Doesberg?

I'd have to say I've never been that curious about art. I know that Frank Stella is tremendously curious and always has been, but the only artist that I was ever tremendously curious about and studied to any great extent was Constantin Brancusi, but that was quite a bit later on. And I saw a lot of Michael Chapman and Barbara Rose, and I was corresponding with Hollis. By this time, Hollis had gone to Washington to be part of the entourage around Ezra Pound at St. Elizabeth Hospital. They were there to keep up Pound's spirits, trying to lighten the burden of his confinement. Hollis was by this time a devout Poundian. Hollis left Washington sometime in the summer of 1957. He came to New York, and I put him up in the small room I had at the Viking Arms. He came with a friend of his, Mark Shapiro, who was a composer. Hollis eventually got a railroad flat on Mulberry Street. It was just one room, and he was living there with Shapiro. In March of 1958, I wanted to have my vacation because I'd been working at Prentice-Hall a year. They said they would not give me my vacation because I was short one day, so I would have to serve another 365 days because I had only served 364. I told them to screw off, and I quit. At this time Michael Chapman was drafted into the army. He had an apartment on Fortieth Street way on the East Side, and I lived off the sublease there for a few months and then moved in with Hollis. So there were three of us living in this tiny place. Hollis had a job at the Renaissance Print Shop in the Village. He was very good at it and made money. He paid the rent—nineteen dollars and eighty-four cents, which I thought was very Orwellian. While I'd been living in the Viking Arms uptown I was doing allegorical drawings and paintings, kind of semisurreal. Not very interesting.

What stimulated that?

I had gotten to the point where doing these things was just one of my pleasures. It seems that the plastic arts were very important to me, far more than literature or the studying of the English language.

But there was still no definite pattern?

No, no, except at various times. When I was in Quincy, either staying there or visiting my parents, I spent a lot of time in my father's workshop with his tools and blocks of wood. I remember as a young man, or as a child, my father used to get loads of timbers, cut-up blocks from the shipyard, and it was my job to split them up for firewood. I remember he had, as well as various odds and ends of wood, a box or a bin of odds and ends of pieces of metal, sort of cut up. There was a section of railroad track and all kinds of blocks and shapes and plates. That material—metals and woods and brick and stone and all these things that I work with now—was always very close to me.

Well, one of the things I did while I was staying at the Viking Arms was a series of drawings, or I started a series of drawings about the adventures of reason and squalor. First was the *Marriage of Reason and Squalor*, then the Flight of Reason and Squalor into Egypt, the Capture of Reason and Squalor by Pirates, and then the Ransom of Reason and Squalor. I think the only one I ever did was the *Marriage of Reason and Squalor.* Then I think I started the Flight of Reason and Squalor into Egypt.

Anyway, when that lease ran out, I went down to stay with Hollis on Mulberry Street, and then I really started doing sculpture in earnest. I started doing small wood pieces from blocks of wood I would pick up on the streets. It involved a great deal of burning and then brushing.

How did you burn the wood?

Just over the stove, I think. The point was, it was a way of modeling into the wood without cutting it. I didn't use a chisel. You just burn an area away, carbonize it, then you brush it away and you get a curved surface. And in plastic. I remember getting plastic blocks. They were very expensive. I had this thing about negative sculpture. What I wanted to do was cut into the body of the block of plastic or block of wood so...

So the form would be contained?

Exactly, concave instead of convex, exactly. Which was a silly idea. But I think that was my response to Brancusi. Because of my closeness to Hollis and Pound's closeness to Brancusi, it was inevitable that my attention should be drawn to Brancusi.

But you would retain the outside forms and flat surfaces–mechanical surfaces?

Right, yes, whatever the external thing was. I suppose this was because I admired Brancusi, and I wanted to do Brancusi, but I didn't want to do Brancusi's Brancusis, so I suppose this was my way of doing *my* Brancusis, because it just reverses the appearance.

Did you read Pound at any point?

Oh, yes, indeed, yes. Hollis had a library of Pound's works and related works, and living with him was Pound and Wyndham Lewis and C. H. Douglas, Alexander Pope.

Did he get into Pound politics and economics, too?

Hollis's interest in politics was entirely poetic. It was Pound's interest without understanding what Pound is talking about—referring to. Whether the economics be sound or crackpot is beside the point; you have to have a certain exposure to grasp the movement of the poems. And Pound was also I think a premier critic of sculpture of the twentieth century.

Really?

Oh, absolutely, he was in London...

Henri Gaudier-Brzeska.

And Jacob Epstein, right, and later on it was Brancusi in France and his...

Carl Andre, *Carved Wood Sculptures*, 1958–1959. *(Courtesy Sperone Westwater Fischer, Inc., New York)*

Very cool forms, generally. He never got anything from Alberto Giacometti.

No, absolutely not, and neither would I. By temperament I really despise Giacometti and that kind of thing. My temperament was drawn very much to the kind of sculpture represented by Brancusi. I remember distinctly the aphorisms of Brancusi, very biblical things.

Have you gotten involved with Sidney Geist and his research on Brancusi? Have you discussed it with him?

No, I'm an enemy of information, because information is just sense experience that passes through somebody else's senses. I'm much more interested in the sense experience that passes through my own senses.

You prefer primary to secondary experience.

Absolutely. My interest in Brancusi was from The Museum of Modern Art and the Philadelphia Museum and the various books, just books of the works of Brancusi, not all of them in English. But I wasn't interested in the text; it was never any help to me. So I started doing sculpture at Hollis's, and at about the same time Frank Stella turned up. He had graduated from Princeton in June of 1958. I would have graduated in 1957 if I had stayed. Frank was dedicated to being a painter.

How did you meet him?

Hollis and Shapiro and I were staying at Mulberry Street, and Frank was staying at Ludlow Street at that time, I think, over on the Lower East Side, and he came by to visit Hollis. I met him then for the first time. I remember the first or second time I met him we went for a walk over the Manhattan Bridge, and, as always, I was scavenging for materials—metal balls and various things like that.

You didn't make assemblages at that point, did you?

Well, in one way all my work is that way, but I never did assemblages...

In the expressionistic sense.

No, not at all. Never, never. I never did a representational or symbolic piece of sculpture after 1955, when I did a few wood carvings. But after that that simply was not an issue. Nor did my work derive from collage, because I really don't derive from painting. My sculptures are of very subjective origin—infantile origin, you might say. I thought dada was cute when I was at Andover.

It didn't hold up.

No, no, no.

And surrealism didn't.

Well, surrealism interested me first as a kind of political and social phenomenon and second as a program for art rather than art. After adolescence, I couldn't take much of Salvadore Dali. Max Ernst is a little better, or more interesting. But dada and Marcel Duchamp I cannot take. I think archness and the utter gentility of the refinement of it all—it's for giggling ladies on the Upper East Side or something. It's salon art.

I believe in the variety of art. That's the only way that art will survive. So I don't say that surrealism should be suppressed or whatever; it just hasn't anything to do with me in any direct sense. I hated plaster even more than clay. I just didn't do that kind of modeling. For me, it was always direct cutting into wood or plastic or...

With what? Saws? Chisels?

Anything. I did a number of pieces in 1959 in Quincy on my father's radial arm saw, the same timber blocks that I used to split up with a chisel when I was a kid. In 1958, when I started working at Mulberry Street, it was drilling into material rather than chiseling. I never was much drawn to the Brancusi organic forms. What I liked very much were the large wooden pieces.

The columns?

Well, *The Endless Column*, certainly. That was the supreme inspiration. I much preferred the regularity of cutting in the bases.

The combination of the wood, metal, and stone?

Exactly. I was much more interested in that than the particular image achieved. It was the whole thing. Much more—the specific gravity of it—the weight, the solidity of it. I have been, like everybody else who showed art in the sixties, associated with minimalism, but if there is such a category as minimalism, which there isn't, I'm about the only one who never made any boxes. It has never been a concern of mine to create volumes. This is not to say that there's anything wrong with volumes, but it's just not in my temperament to go that way. I've always been towards solids.

Anyway, I met Frank Stella and, after having seen him a couple of times, he took me over to his loft, which was tiny—a walkup place, a narrow place. It had been a tiny jewelry factory and it had a gigantic safe halfway down the room. Frank showed me the colored stripe paintings, the stripe paintings before the black ones, very beautiful paintings. I looked at them and thought that Frank was a lunatic. I thought he had probably gone off the deep end, because my idea of art was still related to some kind of abstraction from something outside of art—it had to be derived from paintings and have that interior logic, but to me they just looked blank. Frank moved shortly after that to West Broadway. Occasionally, Hollis and Frank would come back with a timber on their shoulders that they'd picked up from some construction site. Frank said I could go over and work in his place when he wasn't there. So I did sculpture there.

When did you begin working there?

The winter of 1958 and 59. Occasionally, on some scraps, I'd do some painting. This irritated Frank very much, till finally he said that if I did any more paintings he was going to cut off my hands. And I asked, "Why? Wouldn't I ever be a good painter?" He said, "Yes, you could be a good painter, but you never will be." And I said, "Why is that?" He said, "Because you're a good sculptor now." The point was that sculpture obviously was what I had been moving toward, quite unconsciously, the whole time—the solidity of sculpture—and so I continued working there.

Would you discuss Ezra Pound as a critic of sculpture?

Pound had an eye for sculpture. He had a natural inclination toward sculpture, the way I do. He is a critic who can appreciate it. Sculpture is definitely a temperament. Certain people are drawn to it. I think most people are not drawn to it. It's nothing to do with gift; it has to do with inclination. What a critic can do is point out something to look at, and Pound pointed out and stressed Brancusi and Gaudier-Brzeska.

I think sculpture is a more primitive form than painting, the way poetry is a more primitive prose. Sculpture, both in the history of the race and the history of the individual—there's something essentially infantile about the sculptural relation to matter. It has to do with the infant differentiating itself from the world. I suppose that is really the point at which sculpture begins—the sense of sculpture. Of course, that's a disaster, because the infant wants to think of itself as continuous with the universe—the infantile omnipotence. It's a disaster when one realizes one is discontinuous. There is the self, and all that is not the self. And sculpture has something to do with that fundamental feeling. Painting comes at a later stage, in the same way that with poetry—birds come close to poetry in their song, but no animal comes close to prose. Prose comes much later. You need poetry in an oral culture because that's how you remember—through rhyme, through meter, through repetition. But in a print culture, when you can refer to a source, then your aim is exposition, and you leave out all the metric devices.

When did you begin using the graph paper in your poetry?

I was consciously writing poetry before I was consciously making sculpture. The grid system comes from using a typewriter to write the poems and, as you know, a typewriter has even spacing on the lines, as opposed to print which is a justified line and has equal letter spacing. A typewriter is essentially a grid. You cannot evade that situation if you use a typewriter.

After exploring the problems of the typewriter, it wasn't free enough, so I went to graph paper and the business of the in-turning lines, where you read one line from left to right and the next from right to left, which is the way all written languages—horizontal written languages—were originally written. Ox-plowing writing. It's written the way the ox plows a field.

Do you feel there's a relationship between poetry–its visual or graphic presentation–and the structures?

Oh, yes, obviously there has to be. I think that certain fundamental forms are similar in themselves: the triangle looks like a triangle, the square a square, a circle a circle. Rather than trying to achieve a certain look, I was using the same underlying abstractions, the same underlying forms, in both—working out of the grid system of the typewriter to the actual grid system of paper in poetry and also using the same kind of system to plan sculptures to try to find elements that would work within a system, which I call the theory of masonry. I think I said that my grandfather was a mason, and I grew up where bricklaying was very highly respected and practiced. The theory of masonry is that, if you divide a task into units small enough, you can accomplish any task. My work is entirely about units that I can handle without risk, through zero motion and zero threat. Richard Serra's work tends to go into the area of maximum threat, maximum physical extension, quite the opposite. He's a person of tremendous force, and his work reflects that very much, whereas I definitely am a person ever driving toward the greatest serenity I can achieve in any situation. Peace and quiet make me happy. My instinct and my pleasure is definitely in another direction. I would not wish to carry out projects that were beyond my capacity or beyond my own experience. I think there are two general kinds of artists: one is an idealist who has dreams and visions and works through models and drawings and replicas slowly, and, through a difficult process, brings this into fruition. But it's definitely going from the visionary to the concrete. My work almost always goes from the concrete to the concrete. It's a translation within the concrete. My tendency is not the raw shape, but the fundamental unit—use that unit repetitively. But I would not be interested in building an arch, because the brick is not an arch. I would be interested perhaps in building a pier, or just a block.

As an extension of the unit?

Exactly. Also, I don't like to use bonding materials, or even to have structural tensions within, because that's not a property of the individual unit. It is not a property of the unit itself to be bonded. You have to apply something. It also makes them much more permanent if they're not bonded, because if they're bonded they can be broken. If they're not bonded they can never be broken, and they can always be put back together again.

How do you decide what materials will be used?

If one sets out to use metal, there are so many available. I have decided I would prefer not to use alloys. Not that the metals that I use are pure, but I want to stay away from bronze and brass (though I have used those metals). I want to do a series of pieces in the pure metals of commerce, as pure as they are.

Why those?

Well, those are the metals—aluminum, steel, iron kind of thing, magnesium, copper, zinc, and lead. These are called the construction metals. They are the common metals of everyday economic life: the ones we see around us and employ all the time. I'm much less interested in imposing a form on the matter than revealing the properties of the matter. We live in a world of replicas, and I try desperately to produce things that are not replicas.

Your attitude toward materials is in some ways very different from the stonecarvers of the late twenties, thirties, and forties in this country. They would find a stone and then see something in it without changing it's natural found shape too much. But you don't really do that.

Right. I had great difficulty working with natural forms. I've tried working in the wilderness, but to me it first has had to go through some manufacturing process. This place is littered with the stuff I pick up off the street. That's a great source. I try to pick up the least interesting shapes I can find. I'm not interested in the specificity of a shape if it's unique. Its specificity is fine as long as it's one of a set of identical specific objects.

How do you decide what the configuration of bricks should be? Is it the space within which you work?

Well, of course, the space. First of all there is a great misconception the critics always have. They think of art as being manufactured in an ideal space that has no dimension. Art is always in a concrete space. So whenever we're talking about a work of art, whether we admit it or not, we're talking about where it is. But for some reason people are automatically aware of that in my work.

Why are they so aware of bricks in a line rather than a painting on a wall?

I think it's obvious that if my work has a content or a subject matter, part of its subject matter is the relationship between an object and its surroundings. I'm asked if I do the work because of the space it was in. That's a question, and I accept that question. But that's a question that you really have to ask every artist, because no one can build a work of art that is bigger than the space it's in. Nor can one make a work of art that's too heavy to be contained in that space. If my work has any virtue, it's more apparent than this, but I'd like to point out that it's true of all works of art, and sculpture especially, and I have consciously tried to avoid doing this in an architectural way—that is, to build a room inside a room. That's a temptation, certainly, to go toward the architectural. And I've found it would lead to confusion. If I were to go into architecture, I would go into architecture pure and simple. I would not like to make sculpture that is useless architecture.

I was in Japan a couple of years ago, and Japanese art had quite a considerable influence on me—Japanese poetry and music and photographs and architecture and carpentry and, of course, the sand gardens of Kyoto and that whole feeling. Somehow I felt much closer to that than to Western art, any kind of Western art.

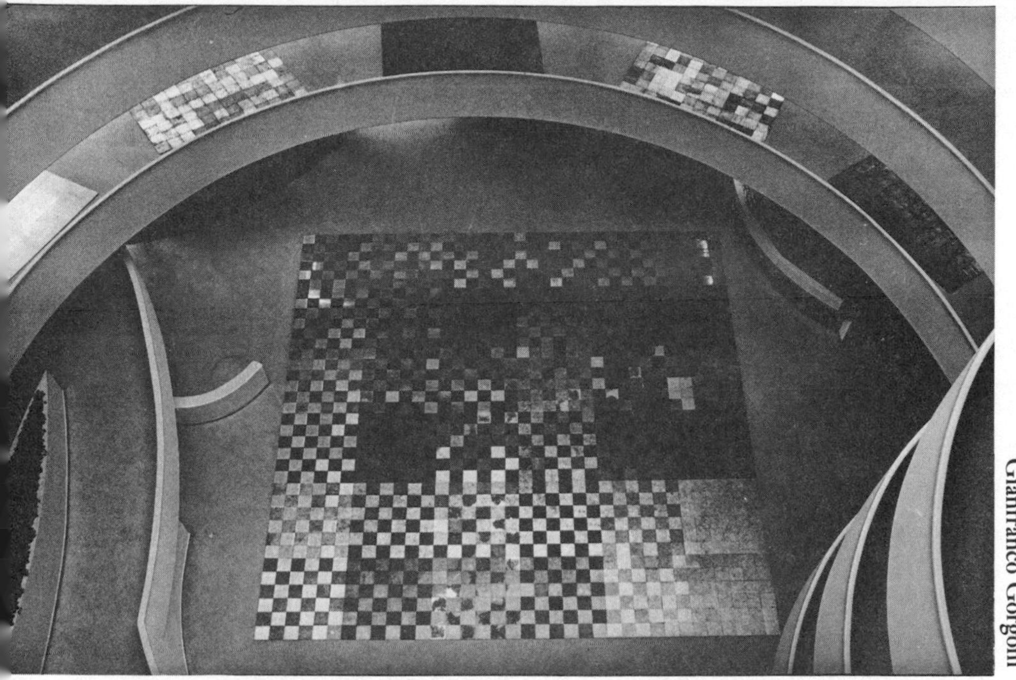

Gianfranco Gorgoni

Installation view of the exhibition *Carl Andre*, 1970, The Solomon R. Guggenheim Museum, New York. *37 Pieces of Work*, 1969. (*Courtesy of Sperone Westwater Fischer, Inc., New York*)

What was the appeal for you?

I have a natural tendency toward calm or rest. Though I found in Kyoto and other places that this kind of calm has to be fierce calm, the calm of a kind of fierce attention, a fierce equilibrium.

What surroundings or buildings or places produce this feeling?

It's difficult to recollect. It's easy to recollect what you felt, but it's hard to recollect which objects and feelings went together. I would say that Jackson Pollock does that to me. One of the big ones like *Blue Poles* or *Autumn Rhythm*—there is something about that space. The paintings of Agnes Martin have it. The paintings of Ad Reinhardt have it. There is a mural at the Metropolitan Museum which I think is the greatest work of art in the city. It's an eleventh-century Chinese Buddhist assembly—the Buddhist's universe—and it takes a whole wall in the Far Eastern room. The first time I saw it, it was as if I were no longer walking on the ground. I was suspended. I felt absolutely levitated. The vision. Some works of art have that for me. I don't think it's because I am a great appreciator of these works or that I have a finer sensibility than someone else. This quality nonsense I just find revolting. It's just that my mental set—my origins, my subjectivity, my history, everything—locks onto a set of stimuli, and my set of stimuli is not going to be the same as somebody else's. There are qualities, and people appreciate different things. I know, for instance, that I'm practically blind to painting. There are very few paintings that move me. Sculpture, even a bad piece of sculpture, interests me. What it's made of. How it was made.

You worked for the Pennsylvania Railroad in the early sixties, didn't you?

From St. Patrick's Day, 1960, to St. Patrick's Day, 1964. These dates have no significance except that it seems, in my life, I have a great turn of fortune in March. I came to New York around February or March; I quit Prentice-Hall I think in March, and, as I said, I went down to live with Hollis in 1958, started working in sculpture seriously for the first time, met Frank Stella, and did my first mature or finished works. The Tate just bought one from that period which was my ultimate carving. I was carving this negative Brancusi-like structure—even *I* called them ladders—and this was an endless column, except it was in concave form rather than convex. I was carving it in Stella's studio on West Broadway. He was admiring its face—it was carved only on one face, the other three faces were not carved. He looked at it approvingly, then walked around it and ran his hand down the back untouched side of the timber, which was about six feet tall, and said, "That's sculpture, too." And it was the side I hadn't cut. I was very much annoyed with that statement at the time and put it in the back of my mind and forgot about it. But my gradual development was to go away from cutting into the material—to use the material itself. So years later I recalled his prophetic remark. I did the wood carving, but the problem of finding timbers big enough—to steal them or whatever, I couldn't buy them—was so difficult, and I wanted to deal with timbers that were thirty-six inches square and you can't get that, so then I started working with two-by-fours, building up criblike forms in a pyramid.

I was a freight brakeman and then a freight conductor. It was a matter of shunting cars around to sidings of industries and making up trains, and as trains would come in breaking them down, classifying them—the operation of making up and breaking down. Drilling it's called, drilling strings of cars. It's very much like my work, anyway. Taking identical units, or close to identical units and shifting them around. But working on the railroad got rid of any ideas of grandiosity in sculpture in my head, because the masses that you're dealing with are so large that—you cannot move a freight car yourself. But it's not strength that allows you to deal with these cars, it's knowing what their properties are and knowing what to do. It's kind of low-level craft—cunning—dealing with the freight cars. But the kind of pleasures of the grandiose—I lost any sense of that there, and it was with great relief that I could deal with things I could trust and manipulate. Things that are unthreatening.

What do you think about the various terms that have been applied to your work–minimal, conceptual, and so on?

Well, minimal I don't mind so much, because in a certain way my work tends to attempt the greatest efficiency with the least means, so to this extent minimal would apply. But to associate with movements—these movements exist only in the imaginations of art critics. An art critic's greatest triumph is to invent a movement. He invents postminimalism, and that's going to be his contribution. As if the original fiction was not phantom enough, he creates the phantom of the phantom. When I was working—there is a great hunk of the 1960s that I left out, because while I was working at the reailroad, people like Bob Morris, Donald Judd, and Dan Flavin were working, and I didn't know any of them. I can't remember having met any of these people before I started showing and meeting them in galleries. I spent a lot of time in the Cedar Bar and Dillons and downtown; there was just no reason for me to go uptown. I do remember in 1960, Frank insisted on taking me up to the Green Gallery to see the Mark di Suvero show, and that really did it. That was a fantastic show. It was fantastic because it broke open the scale problem.

In what way?

Well, sculpture for me was still confined to, if not an actual pedestal, a phantom pedestal, in a manner of speaking.

It wasn't on the floor?

It could be on the floor, but I guess I was still pretty much locked into the monolith, or cutting into the monolith. And the Mark di Suvero pieces were sprawling. I suppose that was the great sense. Even the phantom pedestal was gone; the floor itself was the support, also the size of the timbers he was using, and there was a kind of roughness and unfinishedness of materials. It was tough strong sculpture. It was most distant from jewelry. The two horrible poles—the ultra violet, the infra red. I think architecture is the infra red of sculpture, and jewelry is the ultra violet of sculpture, and you've got to stay clear of those two extremes. The only good strong hard sculpture around at that time was David Smith's, and I knew I was never going to do David Smiths or anything like David Smiths. But with Mark it was sort of wide open. Oh, and while I was working on the railroad I wrote a lot of poetry, did very little sculpture, again because of being broke and not having the time or the place to do it. My work has always sprung from scavenging from the world, finding in the world the concrete matter. It's in the tradition of direct cutting. It's the ultimate absurdity of direct cutting in the world, and that's where it comes from. The other methods have just been eyewash to one degree or another. The only so-called drawings or anything like drawings I do now that are related to sculpture are just deeds of insurance to go along with a piece, so the person can be assured that since I won't sign a piece (it's ridiculous signing a block), I will put my mark on a piece of paper. That assures the person that this is indeed a work of Carl Andre, that he recognizes it's a work of his and so does the collector. But that's just a configuration of the piece, it's not a drawing of the piece.

I happen to disclaim any association with ideas in my art whatsoever, and a favorite line I like to quote is Dr. Joseph Ignace Guillotine's, the eighteenth-century philanthropist, who said all ideas are the same except in execution. And to me the work of art is not the embodiment of an idea; it doesn't spring from an idea; it has nothing to do with ideas. Ideas are abstractions of a different order than works of art. They are not only of a different order, but they exist in a different kind of space. Ideas by their very definition exist in zero space. And you can think about art objects, you certainly can, you can make ideas from art objects, but you can't make art objects out of ideas, because the translation does not work in that way.

The art object serves as a catalyst?

No, I'm not sure what the art object serves as. It serves more as a locus, I think, a locus of attention, a stimulus. I've been associated recently, quite involuntarily, with a grim misreading of my work with the development called "art as idea" or "conceptual art."

There is a magazine in England being published now that has to do with language. . .

Art and Language, yes, I know. I've met those people.

What do you think of that linguistic development as opposed to art?

I think it's a fallacy to begin with; it's a linguistic fallacy and an aesthetic fallacy. Art is not a language system. What this is is a form of disguised religion, and the people who espouse it are quite unaware that it is a form of disguised religion. The reason I say that is because they say that art is language because everything is language. Finally they have to propose that the universe is a language. It is written by who? For what? Well, of course, it must be written by the divine hand as a prophecy to its chosen people. That really is what it is when they say "art and language." It's a spiral. If you start with that small generality, then you must continue it. They're interesting people to a great extent, but they can talk to me about art, and I can't understand a word they are saying. Now one of three cases is true: what they are saying is nothing but jargon, which it sounds like to me; or it is a complex discourse in a discipline I do not understand—it has no application to me, which is possibly true; or it may be so profoundly revealing of art, something which I know a little bit about, that it completely eclipses my understanding. Any one of those is possibly true. I fear it is the first or the second case.

Don't you feel some of those people fall into concrete poetry in their use of language?

Oh, I wish they did. There is not a Gertrude Stein among them. I'm a great admirer of Gertrude Stein, and there is not one among them. A lot of it sprang from Ludwig Wittgenstein. There was a point in the early sixties when everybody had *The Blue Book* and *The Brown Book* in the john. Wittgenstein is interesting, but essentially he is a very shallow philosopher. I've read little or nothing of him; he is not the kind of philosopher that interests me. I've just picked up on a thirty-five-cent remainder shelf the *Life of Reason in Art* by George Santayana, and this is quite another thing. I admire what Santayana writes about art, because it reads very much like my own thoughts, except more well-ordered and better expressed. And Santayana is no analytical philosopher at all—he's an observer; he makes observations and comments. This book was written in 1905, and it's a description of work that I'm doing today.

Cubism wasn't even established. *Les Demoiselles d'Avignon* had not even been painted then, but it's sufficiently abstract so it's a formulation that almost any kind of art work that works, that has power, can be described in this method. It is not so general as to be useless. I do not believe that art is the same as language. Though art obviously has linguistic aspects, I certainly would agree with that. But art is no more language than the universe is language than matter is language. Matter is not language, and if somebody hits you over the head with a club, he's not trying to tell you something, he's trying to kill you, and that's not a message.

Art has to do with early sexual traumas and weaning and toilet training and reading. Learning to read, I guess, is the third infantile sexual trauma, and some people never get over it. They want to read the universe, which is the religious desire. I don't think that art can be done in the mind, and I don't think art exists in the mind, and I don't think it's experienced in the mind. It's a more total thing; it's experienced with the body and the organs of sense and sight.

Do you think our Puritan heritage makes it difficult to experience things that way, or to talk about them?

There's a great resentment. That was my upbringing. One of the great objections to art was the fact that it had something to do with sex. Obviously, art is sexy in its basic root. It is about an erotic relationship with the world, and that's the aspect. Though thought can be sexy absolutely, and working on a mathematical problem can be deeply satisfying and all that, to isolate it, to make file clerks out of artists... There is no reason why a file clerk can't be an artist in filing his cards, but to say that that is the *whole* art! Of course, that is the fad. A few years ago it was structuralism. Claude Levi-Strauss was king. And who was the latest? Noam Chomsky, and Chomsky is going out of fashion. I hate to see this intellectual faddism come and go with my own work.

Lucas Samaras, photograph by David Gahr, c. 1968 (*Courtesy of David Gahr*)

LUCAS SAMARAS

11

The small, but ancient town (it dates to about 500 B.C.) of Kastoria, Greece, was the birthplace of Lucas Samaras in 1936. He lived in a house of women—his mother, two aunts, and a grandmother. His father, who was working in the United States, remained there when World War II was declared. Samaras remembers the shifting armies, the bombings, the military games of the children, parades, privation, and a childhood of chance and wonder. In 1948 he came with his family to join his father in America.

When confronted by a new language and country, alienation often results in solitude. To the curious mind, solitude occasionally suggests reading as a private way to experience. With language a temporary barrier, Samaras expressed himself by making marks on a page. He began to formulate an art of transformed memories, stated and restated in a changing panorama of materials.

It was by chance that he won a scholarship to Rutgers University. During his second and third years there, he became friendly with two people who would become important influences: Allan Kaprow and George Segal. "Allan is verbal, not really capable of working with his hands as a craftsman. Whereas George liked to work with his hands. Even his plaster—he likes to feel it." Samaras found provocative the conflict between idea and craft and incorporated it as a catalyst in his own work.

This interview, begun on January 18, 1968 at the artist's apartment-studio, has been excerpted from a transcript of 104 pages. Biographical interviews convey not only facts, but ideas, attitudes, something of the cultural climate in which the subject lives, the concerns of popular or arcane thought. Rarely, if ever, do interviews suggest the answer to the riddle of an artist's work. If they do, we then confront only illustration. Samaras wished to create "an art that would be of wonder and horror" and to broaden the variety of materials available to make art. The compelling evocations with which he imbues his images are informed by byzantine colors and memories of the incense-laden religious rites he experienced as a child. They are often suggestive of ritual. He utilizes tesserae of experience displayed in bold graphic terms charged with suggestion. He is fascinated that in art he can "materialize a dream."

In 1957 I first began doing things that I am not ashamed of, that were mature enough to be shown anywhere. I am talking about pastels. I was going to raise pastel to the prominence of painting.

Have your pastels been shown anywhere?

I showed them in 1959 at the Reuben Gallery and subsequently at the Green Gallery.

How did you select pastel?

It's something that has to do with me. I don't know. I did pastels in high school, and I still have one. I did watercolors in high school, too, but pastel—the chalk must have attracted me for some reason or other. Also, there were two colors in pastels, red and a blue. I suppose it's ultramarine blue, I am not sure. Or cobalt blue. The blue and the red absolutely sang on a page.

Were they on black paper or colored paper?

I used colored papers in the beginning. I guess construction paper came both in colors and in black and white, so you could have whatever you wanted. Later I began using more and more black, but in the early days I used color. And I would leave some of the paper exposed.

Were most of the pastels small?
Yes. All of them were small. It was a nice thing because I would work on my lap most of the time, on a piece of board, and I would do a batch—three, four, five, up to seven, let's say—at a sitting or in a day.

Did you make people images?
People or stripes.

What kind of stripes?
I was using stripes mostly on backgrounds, as a background curtain. Then on the foreground I would put an object like a flower pot. The stripe itself would be a repetition. It would be blue, green, yellow, blue, green, yellow, blue, green, yellow.

Up and down the whole painting?
Yes. Up and down. So it would follow diagonally. It would be repeated. How can I say it? It was a geometric thing, but it also looked like a curtain, you see. So it was a two-thing.

The pastel was soft?
It was soft, yes.

So you could have a "fabric" kind of feeling?
Then I did some that had nothing else, just stripes.

In color sequences?
A color, then silver, a color, then silver. Silver was interesting.

How did silver become important?
When I first hit upon it, I said, "My God, nobody is using silver. I am going to introduce silver into art." See? And I did some, and they were astounding—the pastels. It was absolutely marvelous.

Do you think it was things you saw when you were young coming back in a new way?

Yes, but who thinks of the old things? You think of today. Fluorescents had come in. I don't know when they had come in, but around 1957 fluorescents were available in small little cans. And I would use those with my...

That was pretty early to use them.

Yeah. They were there. And after I would use them, I'd think: My God, nobody has used fluorescents before. What is amazing is that that kind of adolescent reaction is exactly the type of thing that happens now, with acrylics and new material.

Oh, yes, stripes. Who was doing stripes? At that time Kaprow was. He would have a figure, and there would be some kind of vague stripes in the background. Hans Hofmann was using stripes as a kind of push-and-pull thrust business.

Well, he used bars and rectangles.

Bars! Well, bars are stripes, aren't they?

Depends on which aesthetic you're using.

But the stripe business probably comes, let's say, in impressionism or in Cézanne. In the background you have a horizon or a table or something, and when the table is intercepted by something in front of it, the plane shifts. The left plane and the right plane are not on the same level. They shift. That is probably one little germ for the kind of activity that the stripe was used for later on.

You were able to produce quite definite images by 1958. Were you aware that your pictures had an individual quality about them? Did you suspect it?

I don't think I could look at myself from that removed a position. All I could tell was whatever I did was something that thrilled me. That, you know, I was either ready to march up and show it to Alfred Barr or I wasn't. Robert Whitman and I did take our work to The Museum of Modern Art.

When was this?

I think 1958. Alicia Legg was the person who was seeing work. She saw it and thought it was very nice: "Come back in a couple of years."

The same old story.

I could have killed her.

What did you show her?

I showed her pastels, and Whitman showed her a little box construction.

Had you made any boxes at that time?

At that time, no.

[After Rutgers] I went to Columbia and came in contact with Meyer Schapiro. And he killed all of my desire to be an art historian by being such a fantastic encyclopedic teacher. After listening to one of his lectures, I thought: My God, I know nothing. How could you? His lectures were never simple, never structurally illuminating. They had bits of information scattered throughout, but you never left feeling that you understood anything. It was ten thousand bits of information that were given to you, and God knows when they would form themselves into something, that is, from the art historian's point of view. Now, being an artist and listening to him at lectures, I felt that he knew as much as any artist knew about art. So that was wonderful. And he had a preference for artists, so if you were an artist with a fair degree of intelligence, he would listen to you with eyes much different from the way he would listen to or look at the art history student.

Why was that?

Partly because he paints on the side. I guess he loves art.

He maintained that fascination about the "What is it?"

I don't know, but the contact with him was very profitable, very good.

How long did you study with him?
Two years. I took a number of courses with him. There was a course on early Christian art and impressionism.

You were still living in New Jersey?
I was living in New Jersey and, at the same time, I was going to Stella Adler's acting school.

How did you pick that school?
I was in one of Kaprow's happenings, and a girl there suggested Stella Adler, because she had studied with her. So I went in and received a scholarship.

Which happening were you in?
That was Eighteen Happenings in Six Parts. And then I decided to go into my other friends' happenings, rather than continuing with Stella Adler. It happened like that.

How did you make that decision?
It probably occurred after having spent a couple of days making the rounds, going to casting agents. They look you up and down, and all of a sudden you become a "thing." Their expressions make you begin thinking that your body is worthless. It is a tremendous thing, being an actor—your body and what you do with it. The kind of reception that you get from secretaries is absolutely—it was terrible, horrible, disgusting.

Why did you make the rounds?
Because I wanted to participate.

Everything was still hinged to the educational experience.
Right, right. Because I had to have absolutely all the information, all the knowledge that was available from the wisest or the most intelligent person. I had to have whatever was available.

So Schapiro was the only one that was really important?
There was nothing else there. Just Schapiro and the slides. And

Installation view of Lucas Samaras' *Bedroom*, 1964, Green Gallery, New York. *(Courtesy of The Pace Gallery, New York)*

the library—that was one nice thing about Columbia. I didn't know anybody. It was a cold place for me.

I would go to the library into a little cell, and there would be nobody there, just me and the lamp and the stacks of books. And I would be reading something about the eleventh century or the ninth century, and that was terrific. Such a feeling of being completely lost.

You could really move out into something else.

That was very nice. But I guess psychologically it was very bad for me, because I would get headaches or terrific hunger pains. I couldn't stand too much of it. I guess it was anxiety.

Did you have any contact with any of the students you knew at Rutgers?
Just Whitman.

But otherwise, Columbia was the end of everything. Would you tell me something about Stella Adler's classes? What happened there?
Probably what was valuable was learning to effectively control my body. Now, what do I mean by that? Having grown up mainly with women at a certain part of my life, naturally I identified or copied some of their mannerisms, or some of, let's say, their way of looking at things. The feminine way of looking at things. And through conversations or the relationships I had with my cousin or other male members of my family and through myself, I was aware of the male way of thinking things. So that it is possible that I grew up knowing a fair amount about both sides. Things that maybe not every kid has a window into. So going to Stella Adler's, I could somehow become aware of fears or difficulties I might have had in dealing with people. And there would be ways of doing things that would somehow create less difficulty. There was a way of exhibiting yourself there. You would exhibit so much that there would be nothing to hide. So that once you went out into the world, they could do anything to you and it wouldn't matter. You wouldn't be crushed.

Do you think it was a kind of group therapy?
Yes, group therapy, but through a long tradition. Through a form, which is acting. Acting is a way of doing things with a long history.

It has its formulas and techniques.
Right, right. And how to effectively use yourself and, by that aspect, use other people.

You found this was useful to you in learning and in real life situations?
Yes, of course. A real life situation. Also, at the same time, I went to therapy for a year. It was a more socially-minded analysis. So the two together were very important.

Is there any particular reason why you decided to spend a year in therapy?

After Rutgers, I was deprived of the communication I had had with my friends. I lived with my parents. And then I quit Columbia. There was little contact. The kind of contact that goes on to four o'clock in the morning. There was no self-analysis anymore. And that is what we did. We analyzed ourselves, everybody else, the world, life.

You must have been quite serious about the theater, since you went to the point of making the rounds.

Of course, I was serious. But I should have stayed longer. My emotional equipment was not quite ready for me to have graduated acting. I lied a little bit. Where I would go into scenes and I would act out a scene or something, I would hide all my faults so Adler wouldn't see them. I should have done the opposite.

Do you think she was aware of that?

Well, at the end, she was hitting too hard.

Ah, that was it. She was getting very close to home.

Right. So I said bye-bye.

Did you get as involved with the acting students as you had with the art students at Rutgers?

No, because, again, the acting students were not as intelligent as the Rutgers students. They were emotional; they had other equipment that was necessary for acting, but not necessarily for an intelligent conversation.

They were more directed than creative.

That's true, too. If I had been at the Actor's Studio, I suppose it would have been more interesting.

You mentioned being in some of the happenings.

I participated in the happenings of my friends. First Allan Kaprow's, and then Whitman became interested in doing them, and with a friend he worked out a funny, gory passage that sort of developed into a happening. After that, he did others that I appeared in. Then I moved on to Oldenburg.

How did being in a happening compare to being in Stella Adler's school?
Being in a happening was like being in something that had never existed before. That is how it seemed then. And I was very good, you know. People liked us. It was our way of making ourselves known artistically. I wasn't doing a happening, but I did my roles, and they were mine. So we were beginning to put our feet into the art world. Or I was, let's say.

Would you say the happenings were new and Adler's theater pieces were old?
Yes. It was the old tradition. You did plays that were written a hundred years ago or ten years ago.

You found the happenings an exciting activity?
Exciting, right. And it was also being with the people you knew, you see; it was also a comradeship. And I guess I was the only one who was studying acting. Because I was an actor (most of the others were just painters), they looked at me a little differently. I had some kind of power.

Did you feel your expereince of being in happenings was quite different from theirs?
Yes. And also it provided me with something I didn't get from Stella Adler. I needed professional recognition. At Stella's you couldn't get it. You would just have her comments. But at the happenings, we would get people from the outside.

The audiences. Did you like them?
They were nice. They were not pretentious. There was a number of people who didn't know the happening, but generally they were friendly. And we would have the regulars who would come.

And see them all?

Yes. And I or somebody else would do something, and the regulars would say, "Oh!" And they really felt. They would see something that would thrill them, and they would sigh or something, and you would think: My God, I got them.

Partly because you were in close proximity.

Oh, yes. Sometimes as close as two feet.

So you could really sense their reactions.

Oh, yes, absolutely. And the kinds of silences that existed. You knew if you had them or if you didn't. These are conventional things that every actor knows, right?

Right.

The happenings provided me with all that pleasure.

You seem to like being involved with a group of people.

Right. It is control. Controlling a number of people. And all that love comes to you and nobody else. It also has to do with challenges. There is a Greek word—*Katorthoma*. It pertains to—it is used in connection with the twelve labors of Hercules. It means a challenge plus a successful completion of a task. Well, that's what was available there.

With the audience.

Right.

You did things with Whitman and Kaprow. What about Claes Oldenburg?

Oh, Oldenburg. Lots of those. All the early ones. I think all of the ones he did in New York.

By that time, he had developed a following.

Whitman and I were very friendly up to around sixty, sixty-one, up to the Reuben [Gallery] days. At that time he didn't know any artists in New York. Through the Reuben, he got to know other people—Jim Dine, Oldenburg, and others. Then we began to see each other in a slightly different light. There was a difference between the kind of happenings Whitman was making and the kind of things Oldenburg was making. Whitman was interested in some of the basic things that both of us were interested in from the time we both started, simple things like walking or running or jumping. And a kind of—yes—isolation. One of the best things he did was where he would run and hit himself against the wall, almost trying to push through the wall. It was a very physical thing, and you saw it right there. The audience was all around you. A very basic thing. Oldenburg was a more social realist kind of artist.

He was also more emotional, I think, than most.

Emotional, yes. But in a sense more conventional, so that, having gone to Stella Adler's, he was really my meat. Because he was involved with characters, you know. He selected fat Henry or skinny Olga or...

They were types and caricatures?

Right. So Oldenburg was easy.

In a sense his happenings had a more literary tradition behind them than Kaprow's did.

Yes, right. Though you can't say that Kaprow didn't come from history, too. But Oldenburg, even his art work, has a basis on things that exist already, which is out of Disney or folk America, etcetera.

You used all kinds of material to make the little boxes, didn't you?

The first box started being just a box that I had put plaster in—plaster and cloth. I was doing some plaster and cloth sculpture at that time. The second box was where I used a mirror. I put tacks on the mirror, and that was for me an echo of a pastel that I had done of a face, where I put speckles of blue paint, blue chalk and the blue sang out. And when I did it with a mirror—the mirror and the tacks—it was the same kind of business only with a different idea. On one side was a mirror with tacks and on the other side was a rag face. And it closed. A lot of people liked it. I liked it. I used hair, you know, a little box full of hair. It looks like pubic hair, but it isn't. It's my mother's natural hair. I did another small box of a cotton finger with a real nail with little colored glass beads inside. You would open it and it would be horrible and fascinating, too.

How do you select the materials?

In the beginning I didn't accumulate anything, it was all accidental steps. I didn't accumulate, but I stole things that were in my house. I used forks and knives or else pins that my mother used. It just happened one day; I picked them up, and I put them in a bunch. And it thrilled me, I guess. So I then went out and bought some more.

Did you plan the boxes?

I would make little drawings sometimes. And then a detailed drawing for the carpenter, because I never built them myself. Or else I found boxes, in which case I stripped them of their ornaments and transformed them.

Had you seen Joseph Cornell's work?

I have vague recollections of his work when it was reproduced in *Art News* in 1956. Whitman had shown me the article; he was more into it than I was. It didn't interest me then. It was only later, after I was doing it, that I began to see his work.

What made you start making boxes?

It just came along, and it seemed absolutely right for me.

Do you have any reason for choosing sharp instruments, like razor blades, knives, and so forth?

Some of these things are unconscious. I just happened to pick them because they must have meant something. I have translated what these things mean, but I don't know if that *is* what they mean.

Was the room in the Green Gallery show a literal translation or was it a created...

It was a created thing. It wasn't literal. I based *Bedroom* on the room I lived in. It was the same kind of close space and the same kind of arrangement. But it wasn't a duplication; just the feeling was. It was the kind of environment I had.

You've always worked where you lived, haven't you?

That is true.

Have you ever thought of having a studio?

No, I never have. A lot of my art and my life was or is a reaction against other people around me. People would say, "Ah, get a studio." And I'd say, "No, I won't." Or they would say, "Paint big." And I'd say, "No, I won't paint big." They would say, "Well, use a brush." I'd say, "No. I will use stones."

Why do you think it happened that way? Were you just being contrary, or did you find it stimulating when somebody would tell you what to do?

Well, it is a desire to create something monumental out of something that other people think is ridiculous.

Or unfashionable, or not used.

Yes, right. But it is only after I find out by going to art history books that the thing I set out to do, which was to revolutionize certain things about art, are not really revolutions. These things have been done before, hundreds of years ago.

Did you find that the art history you studied changed your work, in the sense that it showed you where an idea had been used before?

Sometimes it happened like that, yes.

Did you find something in ancient art that you felt was incomplete, that you felt should be redone your way?

Well, that is a strange phenomenon—this business of creating something in 1966 that is perfect for 1966 or 1967 or 1968. What is important here is invention. I think the mistake of all the critics today is that they look at art and say, "Oh, my God, he invented that!" But they don't go back enough in history. If they did they would say, "No, he didn't invent that, somebody else invented that." Now, on the other hand, that doesn't mean that art doesn't change. So if somebody did a square in Roman times, as part of a wall decoration, just a square, and [Kazimir] Malevich did it or somebody else, it is different. But you can't say that Malevich invented the square. I mean, did he? I don't know. What was I thinking about? Oh, yes, the kind of illusions one has when one comes out of school—that one is going to take over the world or do something that has not been done before.

Do you think it is possible?
It is possible when you take the total art work of your lifetime. Then it is possible to do something that nobody else has done. What excited me recently is the Picasso show.

The Sculpture of Picasso [*MOMA, 1967*].
And there were small things, humble things. And some grand things. The things that he did with paper, just taking a piece of paper and cutting out a monkey face—that is wonderful. That kind of dialogue I am interested in.

Material and ideas.
With materials, and also with dead people or with dead art.

In what way, dead art?
I mean art that has been done already.

You've always had the feeling that art was something you had to struggle for, haven't you?
Oh, yes, because it has to do with the mastery of the hand. In order to translate what the brain thinks, you have to have mastery of your extremities.

So you realized there was craft involved.
Oh, absolutely. Yes.

As well as imagination?
Well, that was easier, I suppose.

The imagination?
Yes, because perhaps that aspect of art—the imagination or the individualness—was more difficult to grasp, so that it came slowly, piece by piece, as I grew up. The greatness was always there. The craft quality was always there. Even as a child, you could see that you needed craft to do it. But the imagination is something very difficult. I don't think you can grasp it as a child. I mean, if somebody says, "Oh, you're imaginative because you do that figure this way," I don't think you can grasp it. You do what you do.

Installation view of Lucas Samaras' *Chair Transformations*, 1970, The Pace Gallery. (*Courtesy of The Pace Gallery, New York*)

Then in youth, one can't really criticize one's work.
Even in college I don't think I understood too well what imagination is. My idea of my own work in relation to other artists was also, I think, sort of immature.

In what way?
I think it has to do with your own individual style, your own individual ways of doing things. You have to develop that in a positive way. You have to begin to think about imagination in relation to other imaginations. It is very difficult. I can't explain it.

Do you think your images, to use a general word, develop out of images from older works?
Well, from my own art historical diggings into my own work, I would say that they develop from past things, yes. There is a continuity.

What were your earliest mature works after the pastels?
After the pastels and those thick paintings, the next phase had to do with plaster. I believe both Kaprow and Segal were urging me to go into plaster, because at that time I was still playing a little bit with clay. But clay was nothing. Well, I thought of it as nothing. I think both George and Allan were playing with plaster at that time, I am not quite sure—around 1958 or 1959. So that I really began to play with it in 1959 or 1960, at my house in New Jersey, in my room. I would put pieces of newspaper on my bed and work on top. It had a quality of being fast, you know, so you could sleep, or being small enough so it could be transported. There was a pillow that was old, and instead of throwing it out, I tore it up and took the feathers out and used it with plaster. That was an astounding thing for me. It was a wonderful thing.

The feathers with plaster?
Yes. Mixed together. It was like a parody of baroque frames. And also it was a parody of something eatable.

Like what?
Because it was like meringue, see?

Oh. The plaster was whipped up with the feathers?
Right.

Isn't there a picture like that with a little image in the middle?
Well, that is the piece at MOMA. And then I would also use plaster inside a box. The box was open. I would put plaster in. It would harden so you couldn't close it again. Of course, for me, the development of the box went into a slightly individual area.

Why were the boxes frozen open?
There was one idea there. It came from my pastels. I did some pastels in 1958 where I would make a face, and sometimes in the process of putting one color on top of another in a pastel, it would get a muddy quality. So when you looked at the piece of paper, a nine by twelve, you saw maybe one area that was good and another area that wasn't good. So then I started to put a solid color or a wash over one part of the face. It's as if you erased the face and also as if you put up a curtain from which a face can peek out. The whole page is taken up by a face, and one or two have a curtain on both sides. There is an image that I have always been fascinated by. That is where, on the rectangular piece of paper, you begin making two lines from each of the bottom corners, and, with a slight curve going upward, they meet at the center of the top line. So it is like two circles meeting or like buttocks, or it's a curtain—a part of the curtain. Somehow you are concerned with that kind of opening. The boxes that had plaster in them had sort of a semiabstract figure of a face there, so when you opened it, you opened a box of plaster that was completely solid, but also a plaster that had sort of an anthropoid quality.

I'm lost.
You're lost where?

You mean once the box is opened . . .
The box *is* open.

So the image is a combination of the open box and...

The open box plus some face looking at you through parted curtains.

And then, well, then the box developed...

So, yes, the box developed by itself. But meanwhile, the plaster—I began coloring the plaster then. I made one where there was a horse, and I colored it with fluorescent paint. A brilliant red, I remember. But it was a terrible horse, so I had to destroy it. I did another one—two plaster hands—out of rag. Rag hands, very crude, holding a hot dog in the middle. And the hot dog was painted red. But then I gave the whole plaster business up and went into liquid aluminum. But I had had a little experience with liquid aluminum or what they call Sculptmetal, which is close. The only difference is that Sculptmetal comes in a can and liquid aluminum comes in a tube and has to be squeezed. And if you squeeze it, you can make a line out of it, or a thick stripe. I used Sculptmetal, because my roommate gave me a can one Christmas. So I covered my Plasticine figures.

Were you still at Rutgers?

No, no. This is all 1961, these aluminum things. Gray—the liquid aluminum and gray probably relate to an earlier period in my pastels, where again, there was a certain color gray that you could put on top of a lot of muddy color, and the gray would remain as it came out of the chalk. It wouldn't mix in. It had a tremendous individual quality that you couldn't destroy.

It covered well.

Yes, that was the incredible thing about gray. So that was one kind of color that really excited me. The other color was the tin foil or the silver. I used silver paint mixed in with oils and would get a very wonderful color that hadn't existed before. Then you have the pins coming in as texture. And the pins were like crumpled tin foil, aluminum foil.

So all the way through, there has been an interest in metallic qualities of various kinds?

Yes.

When did you begin using pins?

Well, I think the first pins were not pins, but little nails that I had stuck in the mirror.

Those little tacks.

Little, small tacks. And the first use of pins occurred in a glass that I had put them in. Then I covered a book—the cover of a book. And there were some I covered entirely.

You really introduced a new element–little sharp objects.

The earliest of those was probably in my show in 1961. I had a piece—a liquid aluminum piece with a long needle, maybe a three-inch needle in the middle—that was really a safety pin that was unsafed.

What about other materials used in the objects?

Some of the materials would take a long time to pinpoint, to say, "O.K., now you are going to come with me, and I am going to use you." Once that happened then, in a number of hours or days, I would develop whatever it was that I wanted to use the material with. And then I would realize that whatever I was doing with this material was somehow connected with some other past thing that I had done. So, if you considered the yarn—what is the yarn? It's just a long, thin stripe of color. And it changes color, and it has pretty much the same thickness that my liquid aluminum stripe things have. So that is a jump of going back to the past for a year or a year and a half or two. And it also goes back to pastels, where I used thin strokes of color.

The stripe?

Yes. Only the yarn is a three-dimensional pastel stripe. It is also a translation from sculpture into painting and painting into sculpture. It is a shift between these two mediums.

The birds that you used, for example.

Why birds? Let me think what the first bird was. I am trying to remember. Birds. I can't remember very far back. I can remember some of the pieces that I did with them. There is one piece that I wanted to do, but I never did, which was a box that on the outside was completely covered with birds—these colorful birds. And then you would open it up, and there would be something else inside. Why use birds? My earliest childhood experience, other than some swallows that had nests below our balcony at home, was in school. I remember in our little story books there was one bird that was a teacher bird.

What kind of bird?

Student birds. In Greek there was the word *populaki*—which a mother or a father, I guess, could use for a son—that means little birds. But it is also an expression that could be used to describe the little boy's sex.

It is a European expression.

A European expression, yes. It is interesting that in England a bird is a girl, whereas in Greece it is the opposite. And feathers. That is another thing. You see, I was using feathers with plaster. And that was the completed bird.

What about the black-and-white photograph of yourself?

The early photographs of my face are photographs that I had taken in connection with my theatrical aspirations, so they're photographs that I would send to agencies and all that. Because nothing happened in that field, I began using them in my art. So, with a slight shift, which is a shift from reality or the world into art, which is fantasy, I have been involved in making my face famous through my art work, rather than my acting.

Doing two or three things at once.

And that amuses you?

What about the x-rays?

I bought some medical books and started looking at them, seeing some of the inside parts of the human body. I decided I wanted to know, to see what I'd look like. So I went to a cousin of mine, Dr. Cristos Pyrros, and had my skull x-rayed. And then I took it and I was disturbed about it for a long time.

What provoked that?

I think what is disturbing is knowing or seeing your body, seeing the kind of cover it has, and knowing that underneath there are all kinds of tunnels and crevices and alleys and bugs and germs and things that exist right under the surface. And how horrible it is. It's as if you were God. You realize that you were the universe, and the universe was made up of suns and atoms and gases and things, and how horrible it is that you are not made up of one thing. You are made up of millions of icky substances. And looking at myself or seeing some things on the x-ray—it was a way of my seeing my bones before I am dead, to see how they would look after I die. It is a way of seeing the future. And seeing myself at that deplorable state, where I won't know, where I won't exist.

But you still had the desire to see?

Yeah, that is part of the greed. I have to experience as much as possible. It is as if only today exists, and why not experience everything that one experiences during a lifetime. The mind should be tuned, should be tightened or screwed to a very high point, where you become extrasensitive about things.

Robert Smithson, *Mirror and Gravel Piece for Cornell University*, c. 1969. The artist at upper center. (*Courtesy John Weber Gallery, New York*)

ROBERT SMITHSON

12

In a short interview on July 14 and 19, 1972, at his New York studio, Robert Smithson (1938-1973) recounts his struggles as a young artist trying to discover his sensibilities and the materials compatible to a personal expression. As a high school student, his initial encounter with professional artists was through Isaac Soyer's son Avram, who took him to his father's studio, where with other students Smithson would sketch and discuss art. Occasionally, they would visit museums. He recalled the identification he felt with the artists represented in Les Fauves, an exhibition at The Museum of Modern Art in late 1952. When he attempted to introduce their ideals and concepts at his high school in Clifton, New Jersey, they were rejected. A series of large woodcuts executed in "a kind of German expressionism" led to a scholarship at the Art Students League, where he studied with John Groth, pursuing his intention to become an illustrator.

Smithson describes his school days, his army service, and the poets, writers, and artists—Hubert Selby, Franz Kline, Alan Brilliant, and others associated with the Tenth Street galleries—whom he met at the Cedar Bar, a haven in Greenwich Village for the abstract expressionists. In reference to the Cedar, Carl Andre is quoted as saying, "That was where I got my education." "In a way," said Smithson, "I kind of agree with him." The effects of his meeting with Federica Beer-Monti, the first dealer to exhibit his work, are discussed in detail.

"I guess the Paterson area is where I had a lot of my contact with quarries, and I think that is somewhat embedded in my psyche. As a kid I used to go and prowl around all those quarries."

Smithson's interest in origins—primordial beginnings, the archetypal nature of things—found expression through his use of the earth as material. His drive to manipulate the earth suggests the landscape artist's ultimate goal, the reconstruction of nature according to man's eye. In the translation of materials into imagery, the sculptor's acute perceptions are sensitively realized. Though he died in a plane crash just as his work was maturing, Smithson's works and ideas continue to be a symbol and a source of inspiration.

How did you meet Federica Beer-Monti?

I took my woodcuts to the Artists' Gallery. It was run by Hugh Stix and his wife. They were very encouraging. In a way, that gave me an opportunity to work for myself. I was the youngest artist to ever show there, and I felt if I could show at age nineteen, I should keep on going. I've always been kind of unteachable, I guess, especially at that point.

The show was reviewed in *Art News* by Irving Sandler, and I just didn't feel satisfied. Strangely enough, the work sort of grew out of Barnett Newman. I was using stripes and then gradually introduced pieces of paper over them. The stripes then got into a kind of archetypal imagistic period, utilizing images similar, I guess, to Jackson Pollock's *She-Wolf* period and Jean Dubuffet and certain mythological religious archetypes.

Did you know Newman's work?

Yes, I saw Newman's work. But emotionally I wasn't—I responded to it, but that latent imagery I mentioned was still in me, a kind of anthropomorphism. I was also concerned with Dubuffet and Willem de Kooning.

Which galleries interested you?

I was very much intrigued by Dick Bellamy's—the Hansa Gallery. When I was still going to the Art Students League, I used to drop around the corner to see Bellamy. He was very encouraging. Also, in the late fifties, I moved to Montgomery Street, about three blocks from him. He was the first one to invite me to an actual opening. I believe it was an Allan Kaprow opening at the Hansa. At the time I was trying to put together a book of art and poetry with Allan Graham (which never manifested itself). Dick had suggested that I go to see the new young artists Jasper Johns and Robert Rauschenberg. I had seen their work at The Jewish Museum in a small show. And also in this book I wanted to include comic strips. I was especially interested in the early issues of *Mad* magazine—man out of control. There was an interesting artist, somebody who had a somewhat psychopathic approach to art. His name was Joseph Winter, and he was showing at the Artists' Gallery. I wanted to include him. I also met Allen Ginsberg and Jack Kerouac at that time. I met lots of people through Bellamy.

At one point you went to the Brooklyn Museum School. Did you like it?

No, I can't say that I really responded that much. I think the strongest impact on me was the Museum of Natural History. My father took me there when I was around seven. He took me first to the Metropolitan, which I found kind of dull. I was very interested in natural history. The whole spectacle. The whole thing. The dinosaurs made a tremendous impression on me. I think that initial impact is still in my psyche. We used to go to the Museum of Natural History all the time.

When did you move to New York?

In 1957, right after I got out of the army. Then I hitchhiked all around the country. I went out West. I visited the Hopi Indian reservation and found that very exciting. Quite by chance, I was privileged to see a rain dance in Oraibi [Arizona]. I guess I was about eighteen or nineteen. I knew about Gallup, New Mexico. I knew about and made a special point of going to the Canyon de Chelly. I had seen photographs of it. I hiked the length of the canyon and slept out. It was the period of the beat generation. When I got back, Jack Kerouac's *On the Road* was out, and all those people were around—Kerouac and Ginsberg, both of whom I met. And Hubert Selby. I knew him rather well; I used to visit him out in Brooklyn, and we'd listen to jazz. I met him when I was sitting at a table at the Cedar Bar. I had read a chapter from his book, and I was praising it to—I think it was Jonathan Williams. It just happened that Hubert was sitting there ("Cubby," as he was called) and, of course, he was very taken with the fact that somebody had liked his story that much.

How did you hear about the Cedar?

I think people just sort of gravitated to it. Tenth Street was very active. Perhaps, again, through Dick Bellamy, or Miles Forst, Dody Muller, people like that. I knew Edward Avedisian, too, at that time. And Dick Baker, who worked for Grove Press, and who became a Zen monk.

You never showed in the Tenth Street galleries, did you?

No. By that time I was even more confused. I had a certain initial intuitive talent in terms of sizing up situations and being influenced. But I had to work my way out of that. It took me three years. I was exposed to Europe through my show at the George Lester Gallery in Rome, which had a tremendous impact on me.

How did that happen?

At the time I really wasn't interested in doing abstractions. I was actually interested in religion and archetypal things, and interested in Europe. I was in Rome for about three months. I visited Siena. I was very interested in the Byzantine. I remember wandering through the old baroque churches and going through labyrinthine vaults. At the same time, I was reading people like William Burroughs. It all seemed to coincide in a curious kind of way.

What was it like being a young American in Rome and having a show?

It was very exciting to me. I was very interested in Rome itself. I wanted to understand the roots of—I guess you could call it Western civilization—and how religion had influenced art.

What had interested you in religion at that point?
I was reading Djuna Barnes's *Nightwood*, T.S. Eliot, and Ezra Pound. There was a sense of European history that was prevalent. And I was very influenced by Wyndham Lewis.

But Pound is not particularly involved with...
He was interested in what Western art grew out of and what happened to it. It was a way of discovering the history of Western art in terms of the Renaissance and what preceded it, especially the Byzantine. I was also interested in a kind of Jungian—I think even in part it was similar to Jackson Pollock's interest in archetypal structures. I was interested in the facade of Catholicism.

Did the results of those interests answer questions for you, or did they pose new ones?
I got to understand the mainspring, let's say, of what European art was rooted in prior to the growth of modernism. It was very important for me to understand that. And once I understood that, I could understand modernism, and I could make my own moves. I would say that I began to function as a conscious artist in around 1964 or 65. I think then I started doing works that were mature. Prior to the 1964 and 65 period it was a kind of groping, investigating period.

What artists were you interested in then?
I was really interested in the past, at that point. I would say that initially the impact was Newman, Pollock, Dubuffet, Rauschenberg, de Kooning, even Alan Davie (whom I had seen, I think, at the Viviano Gallery)—the whole New York school of painting. I felt very much at home with that when I was in my late teens. But then I rejected it all in favor of a more traditional approach. And this lasted from, maybe, 1960 to 1963.

Why did you reject those attitudes?
I just felt that they were—they really didn't understand. First

of all, anthropomorphism, which had constantly been lurking in Pollock and de Kooning—I always felt that a problem. I always thought it was somehow seething underneath all those masses of paint. And even Newman in his later work still referred to a certain kind of Judeo-Christian kind of value. I wasn't that much interested in a sort of Bauhaus formalist view. I was interested in this archetypal gut situation that was based on primordial needs and unconscious depths. And the real breakthrough came once I was able to overcome this lurking pagan religious anthropomorphism. I was able to get into crystalline structures in terms of structures of matter and that sort of thing.

What precipitated that transition?

I felt that Europe had exhausted its culture. I suppose the first inklings of a Marxist view began to arise, rather than trying to reestablish traditional art work in terms of the Eliot-Pound-Wyndham Lewis situation. I just felt there was a certain naïveté in the American painters, good as they were.

Did you get interested in Marxism as a . . . ?

It was just sort of a flicker. I began to become more concerned with the structure of matter itself—crystalline structures. The crystalline structures gradually grew into mapping structures. I gave up painting around 1963 and began to work plastics in a crystalline way. I began to develop structures based on a particular concern with the elements of material itself. This was essentially abstract and devoid of any kind of mythological content.

There were no figurative overtones?

No, I had completely gotten rid of that problem. I felt that Jackson Pollock never really understood that. And, though I admire him still, I still think that that was something that was always eating him up inside.

When did you begin your departure from traditional imagery and your involvement with natural materials?

That began to surface in 1965 and 66. I consider that my emergence as a conscious artist. In 1964, 1965, 1966, I met people who were more compatible with my view—Sol LeWitt, Dan Flavin, and Donald Judd. At that time we showed at the Daniels

Gallery. I was doing crystalline-type works, and my early interest in geology and earth sciences began to assert itself over the whole cultural overlay of Europe. Out of the defunct class culture of Europe, I developed something that was intrinsically my own and rooted to my own experience in America.

What was it about the crystalline structures that stimulated you?

I think it goes back to my earlier childhood responses, a direct response to—I have always been interested in collecting rocks and I had a rather large collection. The first thing I wrote was in 1966 for *Harper's Bazaar.* The article was called "The Crystal Land," and it was about a journey to New Jersey to a rock quarry with Donald Judd.

Gradually I recognized an area of abstraction that was really rooted in crystal structure. I guess the first piece that I did was in 1964. It was called the *Enantiomorphic Chambers.* I think that was the piece that really freed me from all my preoccupations with history. I was just dealing with grids and planes and empty surfaces. The crystalline forms suggested mapping. And mapping—if we think of an abstract painting, for instance, like Agnes Martin's, there's a certain kind of grid that looks like a map without any countries on it. I began to see the grid as a mental construct of physical matter, and my concern for the physical started to grow. And right along I had always had an interest in geology.

I think the interest in geology developed out of my perception as an artist. It wasn't predicated on any kind of scientific need. It was a kind of an aesthetic. Also the entire history of the West was swallowed up in a preoccupation with notions of prehistory and the great prehistoric epochs starting with the age of rocks and going up through—the Triassic and the Jurassic, and all those different periods subsumed all the efforts of the civilizations that had interested me.

What was happening just prior to the grid-system idea?

I made drawings. Kind of phantasmagorical drawings of cosmological worlds somewhat between William Blake and, oh, a kind of Boschian imagery.

Robert Smithson, *Slate Circles on Flat Plain (2 Circles)*, pencil on paper, 16'' x 24'', 1972 *(Courtesy John Weber Gallery, New York)*

There were still figurative overtones?

Oh, very much, yes. Definitely. They were sort of based on iconic situations. I think I made those drawings around 1960 and 61. They dealt with explicit images like the city. They were kind of monstrous as well, like great Moloch figures. They consisted of many figures involved in a kind of — they were almost proto-psychedelic in a certain way. That freed me. The whole notion of anthropomorphism was done away with. I got that out of my system.

And the grids appeared in . . .

It was more of a crystalline thing—more of a triangulated situation. I started using plastics.

Why did you pick plastics?

There was an interim period when I was doing a kind of collage-writing situation, writing paintings.

Like William Burroughs's cut-and-paste poetry?

Yes, well, not exactly. There was a show at the Castellane Gallery that sums it all up. I started working from diagrams. I would take an evolutionary chart and paint it in a somewhat Johnsian manner. But it was a very kind of confused period around 1961 or so.

Several years later you got involved with the Dwan Gallery. How did that happen?

How *did* that happen? I met Ad Reinhardt in 1963 or 64. I was doing the plastic paintings—the crystalline paintings—and I had started to get more into the serial structures that I showed at the Dwan in 1966. Reinhardt asked me along with Robert Morris to help organize a show at Dwan—the 10 Show. Then I did a piece called *Alogon*. The one the Whitney owns now. It was like seven inverted staircases. Also around that time, I had a lot of dialogues with Sol LeWitt and Donald Judd. A lot of things began to pull together around that time. Prior to my going with the Dwan Gallery, I showed the *Enantiomorphic Chambers* that Howard Lipman owns. That impressed Virginia Dwan; right after I showed in the 10 Show, she asked me to be in the gallery. In 1965, I gave a talk—"Art in the City"—at Yale, with Brian O'Doherty and John Hightower. I guess a lot of my thinking about crystalline structures came through, because I discussed the city in terms of a crystalline network. An architect from Tippetts, Abbett, McCarthy and Stratton was sitting in the audience, and he asked me if I would like to participate in the building of the Dallas-Fort Worth Airport, in terms of trying to figure out what an airport is. So I invented this job for myself as artist-consultant. For about a year and a half, from 1965 through 1966, I went there and talked with the architects. That's where the mapping and the intuitions of the crystal structures really took hold, where one is dealing with grids superimposed on large land masses. The inklings of the earthworks were there.

What kind of association did you have with the architects?

Most of the building was done through computers. I was looking at the layout of the airfield. My final proposal was something called "aerial art," which would be earthworks on the fringes of the airfield that you would see from the air. They provided me with all the mapping material. And we had interesting discussions. I made models of possible airports. I became less and less interested in the actual structure of the building and more interested in the processes of the building and all the different preliminary engineering things—the preliminary aspects of building. For instance, the boring of holes to take earth samples. I later wrote an article called "Toward the Development of an Air Terminal Site" [*Artforum*, June 1966], speculating on the different aspects of building.

You were involved with them on a theoretical . . . ?

I was involved with them on a theoretical level. In 1966 I showed a model at the Dwan for a tar pool in a gravel enclosure. I would say that it was mainly theoretical at that time. But right along, right from that point, around 1966, there was an inkling or an intuition that earthworks might be an interesting area to get into. I had also suggested to the architects that they let Robert Morris and Carl Andre and Sol LeWitt do something, and they each presented proposals, which I included in the aerial art program. I wanted to do a spiral, a triangulated spiral made out of concrete. And there were other projects. There was another spiral, a kind of reflecting pool—a basin.

Where did you meet Morris?

I met him during the meetings for the 10 Show. Then I met Don Judd through Dan Flavin. I did show a light piece with mirrors in 1963—my only light piece; it was a curious work. I made it in 1963. I showed it in an exhibition called Current Art, where I met Dan Flavin.

Have you become involved in mathematical structures, or mathematical ideas concerning crystalline structures?

Not really. Well, the title *Alogon*, the piece I showed in the 10 Show, comes from the Greek word which refers to the unnamable and the irrational number. There was always a sense of ordering, but I couldn't really call it mathematical notation. There was a consciousness of geometry in an intuitive way. But it wasn't in any way notational.

It was really the shapes that were . . .

It was, yes. A sort of lattice structure that could be conceived of in a kind of crystalline way.

In the late sixties many artists were working outdoors.

There was always a leaning toward public art. But it still seemed to to be linked somewhat to large works of sculpture in plazas in front of buildings. And I became interested in sites. In a sense, these sites had something to do with entropy. I became interested in low-profile landscapes once again—the quarry or the mining area, which we call an entropic landscape, a kind of backwater or fringe area. There were all kinds of material that broke down the usual confining aspect of academic art.

I was also interested in a kind of suburban architecture: plain box buildings, shopping centers, that kind of sprawl. And I think this is what fascinated me in Rome, just this kind of collection, this junk heap of history. Here, we were confronted with a kind of consumer society. There is a sentence in "The Monuments of Passaic" [*Artforum*, December 1967] where I said, "Hasn't Passaic replaced Rome as the Eternal City?" There is a feeling of an almost Borgesian sense of passage of time and labyrinthine confusion that has a certain kind of order. I was looking for that order, an irrational order that developed without any design program.

It becomes an alteration of nature, doesn't it?

That's something that I think, in the course of one's preoccupation with abstraction—the tendency toward abstraction— is lodged in books like Wilhelm Worringer's *Abstraction and Empathy* [1908], where the tendency of the artist was to exclude the whole problem of nature and just dwell on abstract mental images of flat planes and empty spaces and grids and single lines and stripes. Right now I feel that I am part of nature and that nature isn't really morally responsible. Nature has no morality.

How do you feel a part of it?

It's as though I were involved in a personal archaeology, going through layers of the last years of civilization, back into the more archaic ones—the Egyptian and Mayan and Aztec civilizations.

I became more and more interested in the stratifications and the layerings. I think it had something to do with the way crystals build up, too. I did a series called *Stratas.* Virginia Dwan's piece is called *Glass Strata*—pieces of glass eight feet long by a foot wide—looks like a glass staircase made out of inch-thick glass; it's very green, very dense and layered. My writing, I guess, proceeded that way. I thought of writing as material to put together rather than as a kind of analytic searchlight.

Did the writing affect the development of what you made?

The language tended to inform my structures. If there was any notation, it was a kind of linguistic notation. So, together with Sol LeWitt, I thought up the language shows at the Dwan Gallery. But I was interested in language as a material entity at that time, as something that wasn't involved in ideational values, as printed matter. The information has a kind of physical presence for me. I would construct my articles the way I would construct a work.

I think it probably relates to a somewhat physicalist or materialist view of the world, which, of course, leads into a kind of Marxian view. So that the old idealisms of irrational philosophies began to diminish. Though I was always interested in Jorge Borges's writings and the way he would use leftover remnants of philosophy, so to speak.

When did you get interested in him?

Around 1965. Taking a discarded system, and using it as a kind of armature. I guess this has always been my world view.

Is it the system that's the valuable aspect or the utilization of it?

No. The system really isn't—it's just a convenience. It's just another construction on things that have already been constructed. So my thinking became increasingly dialectical. I was still working with the resolution of the organic and the crystalline, and that seemed resolved in dialectics for me. And so I created the dialectic of site and nonsite. The nonsite exists as a deep three-dimensional abstract map that points to a specific site on the surface of the earth. And that's designated by a mapping procedure. And these places are not destinations; they're kind of backwaters or fringe areas.

How do you arrive at those different areas?

I don't know. I guess it's a tendency toward a primordial consciousness—toward the prehistoric—after digging through histories.

Do you work from a large map or from memory?

Well, a lot of the nonsites are in New Jersey. I think that those landscapes embedded themselves in my consciousness at a very early date, so that in a sense I was beginning to make archaeological trips into the recent past to Bayonne, New Jersey.

It was a real place that became abstracted to a nonsite?

Yes. And which then reflected the confinement of the gallery space so that, though the nonsite designates the site, the site itself is open and unconfined and constantly being changed. And the purpose was to bring these two things together. And, to a great extent, that culminated in *Spiral Jetty.* But there are other smaller works that preceded that—the investigations in Yucatan.

How did that come about?

Here was an alien world, a world that couldn't be comprehended on any rational level. The jungle had grown up over these vanished civilizations. I was interested in the fringes around these areas. The backwater sites, again, maybe, maybe a small quarry, a burnt-out field, a sand bank, a remote island. I found that I was dealing not so much with the center of things, but with the peripheries. So I became very interested in the dialogue between the circumference and the middle, and how those two things operated together.

John A. Ferrari

Installation view of the exhibition *Mirror/Salt Pieces From Cornell 1969, April–May 1976, John Weber Gallery. (Courtesy of The John Weber Gallery, New York)*

Aren't most of the sites in the country?

Most are in New Jersey. There's one in Bayonne, one in Edgewater, one in Franklin Furnace, one in the Pine Barrens. Since I grew up in New Jersey, I was saturated with a consciousness of that state. And then, strangely enough, the other ones—I did a double nonsite in California and Nevada, so I went from one coast to the other. The last nonsite is one that involves coal; the site belongs to the Carboniferous Period, so it no longer exists. It is completely buried. There's no topographical reference. It's a submerged reference based on hypothetical land formations from that period. The coal comes from somewhere in the Ohio and Kentucky area, but the site is uncertain. That was the last nonsite. That was the end of that. I wasn't dealing with the land surfaces.

How did the idea of sites and nonsites develop?

I began to see things. I began to question very seriously the whole notion of Gestalt, the thing in itself, specific objects. I began to see things in a more relational way. I had to question where the works were, what they were about. The very construction of the gallery with its neutral white rooms became questionable. I became interested in working, in a sense, bringing attention to the abstractness of the gallery as a room, at the same time taking into account less neutral sites that would be neutralized by the gallery. So it became a preoccupation with place.

INDEX

NOTE: numbers in italics refer to illustrations